DELIUS

THE PARIS YEARS

BANKS
MUSIC
YORK

Overleaf: Frontispiece

Delius in 1888

DELIUS

the Paris years

Lionel Carley

TRIAD PRESS

1975

text © Lionel Carley 1975

Delius's songs *Chanson de Fortunio* and *Nuages* © The Delius Trust 1975
Extract from Delius's opera *The Magic Fountain* © The Delius Trust 1975

Typography and layout © TRIAD PRESS 1975

PRINTED IN WALES

CONTENTS

(Main section of illustrations between p 37-44)

ILLUSTRATIONS

Grateful acknowledgement is made to the sources given below:

Frontispiece: Delius in 1888, photograph, Delius Trust Archive; **p 16 André Messager,** caricature by Gabriel Fauré, reproduced by kind permission of the Music Department of the Bibliothèque Nationale, Paris (Jean-Michel Nectoux); **p 21 Ville d'Avray: Corot's lake,** photograph (1973) L Carley; **p 23 8 boulevard de la Mairie, Croissy,** photograph (1973) L Carley; **p 35 A page from 'Anatomie et Physiologie de l'Orchestre'** by Delius and Papus (Paris, Chamuel 1894); **p 37 Papus,** portrait, unattributed and undated, in Philippe Encausse: *Papus, Dr. Gérard Encausse, sa vie, son oeuvre* (Paris 1932); **p 38 Theodor Delius,** oil on canvas, n.d., artist unknown, photographed by Haeyn-Wilms, Bielefeld, and reproduced by kind permission of the Familienverbindung Delius, Bielefeld (Archivist, Uta von Delius); **p 39 13 rue de la Grande Chaumière: Madame Charlotte at the window above her crémerie,** photograph (c. 1900) in the Carlheim-Gyllensköld Collection, Royal Library, Stockholm; **p 40 (i) A Gauguin 'at home' in the artist's studio** (with Sérusier), photograph (c. 1895), in Gilles Gérard-Arlberg: 'Nr 6, rue Vercingétorix', *Konstrevy,* 35,2, Stockholm 1958; **(ii) Ida in the Molards' studio at 6 rue Vercingétorix,** photograph, n.d., reproduced by kind permission of the late Dr. Gerda Kjellberg; **p 41(i) Portrait of Molard** by Paul Gauguin, oil on canvas (c. 1894), from a photograph reproduced by kind permission of the late Dr. Gerda Kjellberg; **(ii) Julien Leclercq,** photograph, n.d., in Julien Leclercq: *La physionomie,* Paris 1896; **(iii) Bergliot Bjørnson,** photograph (1886), in Bergliot Ibsen: *The Three Ibsens,* London, Hutchinson 1951; **(iv) Portrait of Slewinski (detail)** by Paul Gauguin, oil on canvas, 54 x 81 cm (c. 1891), reproduced by kind permission of the National Museum of Western Art, Tokyo; **p 42 'A Fritz Delius: souvenir d'amitié & de vive sympathie—G. Daniel de Monfreid, Fév. 93.'**pastel, 72 x 61 cm, reproduced in *Frederick Delius* (Catalogue of the Centenary Festival Exhibition), Bradford and London, 1962, coll. Mrs Derek Hudson; **p 43(i) 6 rue Vercingétorix,** photograph (1912) Rafael Radberg, in the Strindberg Collection, Royal Library, Stockholm; **(ii) Portrait of Jacques Arsène Coulangheon,** woodcut, n.d., by P-E Vibert, 'after Judith', in Jacques Arsène Coulangheon: *Lettres à deux femmes,* Paris 1908; **p 44(i) Isidore de Lara,** detail from photograph (1890), in Isidore de Lara: *Many Tales of Many Cities,* London, Hutchinson, n.d.; **(ii) Alphonse Mucha,** photograph (1897), reproduced by kind permission of Jiri Mucha; **(iii) Georges-Daniel de Monfreid: Self-portrait,** oil on canvas (1901), also known as 'Portrait de l'artiste—l'homme à la chemise bleue', reproduced by kind permission of the Musée d'Art Moderne, Paris; **(iv) Jean Richepin,** photograph, n.d., in Julien Leclercq: *La Physionomie,* Paris 1896; **p 46 Portrait of Gauguin** by Judith Ericson Molard (Judith Gérard), etching, n.d., in Gilles Gérard-Arlberg: 'Nr 6, rue Vercingétorix'; **p 51 William Molard,** photograph, n.d., reproduced by kind permission of the late Dr. Gerda Kjellberg; **p 53 Portrait of August Strindberg (detail)** by Edvard Munch, lithograph (1896) (Oslo Kommunes Kunstsamlinger), reproduced by kind permission of Curator Gerd Woll, Munch Museum, Oslo; **p 55 Florent Schmitt,** woodcut, n.d., in André Coeuroy: *La Musique française moderne,* Paris, Librairie Delagrave 1922; **p 56 Maurice Ravel,** photograph (c. 1902), in Gilles Gérard-Arlberg: 'Nr 6, rue Vercingétorix'; **p 57-58 Two pages from Ravel's transcription of 'Margot la Rouge':** Ravel's autograph manuscript vocal score is in the Delius Trust Archive, London (Volume 20); **p 64 Portrait of Jelka Rosen** by Ida Gerhardi, oil on canvas, 32 x 25 cm (1897); reproduced by kind permission of the owner, Frau Malve Steinweg, Lüdenscheid; **p 66 Edvard Munch: Self-portrait (detail),** lithograph (1895) (Oslo Kommunes Kunstsamlinger), reproduced by kind permission of Curator Gerd Woll, Munch Museum, Oslo; **p 69 Portrait of Fritz Delius** by Christian Krohg, drawing (1897), in *Verdens Gang,* Christiania, October 1897; **p 72 Delius in 1899,** photograph reproduced courtesy Christopher Brunel (© 1975); **Appendices: Chanson de Fortunio** (Delius—Alfred de Musset), in the composer's autograph manuscript (Croissy 1889), and **Nuages** (Delius—Jean Richepin), in the composer's autograph manuscript (1893): both songs are in the Delius Trust Archive (Volume 36); **p 96 6 rue Vercingétorix,** photograph (1969) R A Unnerbäck, reproduced by kind permission of Göran Söderström.

Thanks are due to the following for processing the illustrations: John MacDougall, Panic (London W1), Tantrums (London W1) and Photographic Service (Music Reproductions) Ltd.

INTRODUCTION

Frederick Delius was born in Bradford, Yorkshire, in 1862, of immigrant German parents who owned a thriving textile firm in that city. He was in fact originally named Fritz, and it was by this name that he was known to his friends for the first forty years of his life, including the period in Paris that is the subject of this essay. As a composer Delius founded no real school, had few imitators and fitted into no easily identifiable stylistic category. He was to make no attempt to compromise with the changes in musical thinking and expression that Stravinsky and Schoenberg, for example, were ushering in at the time of his own period of high maturity. He remained his own man, original, alone. Sensuous, but strong-willed, he lived life to the full, and yet had a marvellous, enviable ability to detach himself at will from fleshly experience, as it were, and to observe and transmute into music moods and impressions, always with a technique that was skilled and assured.

Virtually all of Delius's biographers have been English and have stressed his English ties and experiences. One or two American writers, notably Jahoda and Randel, have recently provided a useful counterbalance, giving more detail than hitherto of the two years in Florida and Virginia that were so important to his early musical development. The period during the early years of the twentieth century when Delius's works were given extensively in the German-speaking countries, where for the first time he became something of a cult figure, has been moderately well documented, even if much remains to be researched in this particular field. But his years in Paris, from 1888 until close on the turn of the century, have been scarcely charted, in spite of their being arguably the most fascinating years of his life—a time when he was on intimate terms with many of the artistic and literary giants of the age.

This account—a prelude to a more extended work—represents a first attempt to record this period, albeit roughly, and with gaps that may perhaps never be filled. As far as possible it moves chronologically, lingering on Delius's more notable friendships as well as on those years which are best documented, either by personal letters to and from the composer or by records of those who knew him or his friends personally. Principal manuscript sources are letters from Delius to Edvard and Nina Grieg, in the possession of the Bergen Library, and from Delius to Mrs. Jutta Bell-Ranske, in the Jacksonville University and Public Libraries, Florida. Letters (originals or transcripts) from Edvard and Nina Grieg, William Molard, Georges-Daniel de Monfreid and Christian Sinding to Delius and from Delius to his wife, all in the Delius Trust Archive, London, have been utilized extensively. A few other letters to Delius, also in the Delius Trust Archive, which are referred to in the text include those from Charles Boutet de Monvel, Emma Calvé, Berthe Gaston-Danville, Gabriel Fauré, Georgette Leblanc, Adela Maddison, Léon Moreau, Achille Ouvré, Maurice Ravel, Florent Schmitt, and Déodat de Séverac.

I am grateful to the Delius Trust, and in particular to the late Dr. Philip Emanuel, for allowing me to publish extracts from these letters and other documents in the Trust's Archive. My thanks are also due to Robert Threlfall, Musical Adviser, and Rachel Lowe Dugmore, former Archivist to the Delius Trust, for advice often sought and willingly given; to Professor William Randel, of the University of Maine, for selflessly making available to me the results of his own researches into aspects of Delius's life during this period; to Mme. Annie Joly-Segalen, Paris, for permitting me to read the diaries of Georges-Daniel de Monfreid that are in her possession; to Dr. Bengt Danielsson, of Papeete, Tahiti, for kind and ready assistance in putting me on the track of documents relating to the Molard circle; to Mrs. Astrid Jägfeldt, Stockholm, who has helped me to trace further documents relating to Delius's Paris period; and, finally, to Mme. A. Merle d'Aubigné for her assistance and hospitality in Grez-sur-Loing during the course of my researches into these early years spent by Delius in France.

Lionel Carley
Paris, July 1973,
London, January 1975.

CHAPTER ONE

The Rue Cambon

and Uncle Theodor

AT THE AGE OF TWENTY-SIX DELIUS EFFECTIVELY emigrated to France. It was a country he had first come to know a few years earlier when he had spent a short time at Saint-Étienne as an agent for his father's wool business. Industrial Saint-Étienne was scarcely likely to endear the country to him, but a few weeks' break on the Riviera, where he developed a taste for the gaming-table, together with a visit to Paris to see his uncle Theodor and something of the sophisticated life-style that he led there, were more than enough to whet Delius's appetite and bring him back to spend the major part of his life in France. Extensive periods of travel were, however, to intervene between the reconnaissance and the protracted stay, and before Delius returned to Paris in the spring of 1888 there had been visits to Scandinavia, to America for two years, and to Leipzig for close on another two years. Indeed, from the age of twenty-two, when his wanderlust first took him to Florida, he had in effect no longer been resident in England.

Dining in London with his friends the Griegs on 4 May, 1888, Delius left for Paris two days later. For his first three months or so in the capital he stayed with his uncle Theodor in the latter's elegant apartment at 43 rue Cambon, where he enjoyed a first real taste of the Parisian social circles in which Theodor Delius moved so urbanely. Theodor numbered the markedly anglophile André Messager among his friends and it was probably about this time that he introduced his nephew to the composer—who was, incidentally, only eight years older than Delius. Messager's greatest compositional success so far had been *Les deux pigeons,* which had received its première in Paris in October 1886, and many musicians—Roussel among them—considered its instrumentation to be masterly. On this point alone one wonders what Delius may have made of Messager's work if, as one may presume is likely, he ever had the score in his hands. Delius must have seen Messager quite often in Paris and quite possibly met Gabriel Fauré around this time too, Fauré being Messager's great *maître et ami*. But there are no letters between Delius and Messager, and almost the only documentary remains of Delius's acquaintanceship with Fauré are letters of introduction to English friends that Fauré wrote on his behalf in 1899.

André Messager:
caricature by Gabriel Fauré

Thanks to a continued allowance from his father, as well as to the benevolence of his sympathetic uncle, Delius was able to live in comparative luxury during this first period in Paris, and he very soon sought out the city's musical activities. The best part of the musical season was now over, but Lamoureux's final concert, consisting of works by Wagner, Saint-Saëns and Bizet, was much to his taste, as was the excellent quality of the orchestral playing, which Delius found far superior to anything Leipzig had had to offer. Then there was *Aïda* at the Opéra, as well as a new work by Lalo at the Opéra-Comique: his unmitigated enjoyment of the first was offset by his disappointment with the second, which he found "quite empty". Delius initially found Paris greatly to his liking. How different the atmosphere of *la ville lumière* to that of its heavier English and German counterparts. All that was missing in fact was the peace and quiet that he knew he needed for work. Not until almost a month had gone by did the opportunity occur seriously to get down to the business of composition: his uncle left for an eighteen-day visit to England, and with him went the social demands of Paris. Delius was really alone for the first time since his arrival, and in what we now know to be typical fashion for him, there, in the centre of Paris, scarcely a stone's throw from the Opéra, in the grave dignity of the rue Cambon, he isolated himself and worked virtually the whole time through until his uncle returned on the 20 June. His production included some songs, the original version of his melodrama *Paa Vidderne* and an unspecified orchestral piece. We cannot with certainty assign to the 1888 songs a strict chronological order. His main output this year was during this particular period in Paris and then in the summer at St-Malo. Seven songs, however, do undoubtedly date from 1888: the *Five Songs from the Norwegian,* dedicated to Nina Grieg and published by Augener in 1892,

Hochgebirgsleben (Ibsen), and *O Schneller mein Ross (Plus vite, mon cheval)*, a setting of a German poem by Emanuel von Geibel. *Traum Rosen*, to words by Marie Heinitz, usually ascribed to 1888, was in fact more likely written some ten years later. It was probably in 1888 too that he made an arrangement of a Swedish folk song (no longer extant), to the delight of the Swedish tenor, Leonard Labatt, a temporary neighbour in Paris, who asked him to arrange some more.

Six weeks were sufficient, though, for the first rapture to wear off. Delius had had some time to sample the luxuries of Paris society, the opera, the Bois de Boulogne criss-crossed by the carriages of the wealthy. But there were two worlds in Paris, and the brilliance of the one only served to throw into sharp relief the wretchedness of the other. As one might expect of a young and enquiring nature, Delius would walk about the streets of the poorer quarters of Paris, a relatively unnoticeable figure when dressed, as he purposely would be, in his oldest clothes. His curiosity took him several times to the Morgue, where the corpses of those who had been murdered or who had committed suicide were laid out, a visit which was one of the more vicarious thrills available in Paris at the time. A degree of disillusionment with the brittle refinement of Parisian culture and society began to set in and manifested itself in various forms. Delius decided, for example, that French music was art and artificiality: "the great vitality of nature" was missing. While acknowledging that he was widening his experience greatly in this fascinating city, he dreamed of the great spaces of his already beloved Norway, of the distant mountains and cool fjords which had so swiftly exerted their spell on him and to which he was to travel so frequently in future years. He had no intention at present of settling in Paris—one day he would make his home in the North.

With Theodor's return to the rue Cambon the luxurious life resumed its course and once again Delius's attempts at composition were greatly hindered by the social obligations that the household imposed on him. Nor is high summer in Paris ever particularly conducive to the creative muse, and before long Delius sensibly quit the capital. Spending the early part of August at home in Bradford he then made his way to Brittany where, based for over two months at St-Malo, he explored some of the Breton coastline and did a great deal of bathing. He managed to get a considerable amount of work done into the bargain: one of his first tasks was to dramatise Bulwer Lytton's novel *Zanoni*, a work first published in 1842 and showing its author's preoccupation with and love for the mysterious; Delius started to write incidental music for it, feeling that it did not lend itself to full operatic treatment. He wrote more songs, revised *Paa Vidderne*, completing the work by early October, and a letter he sent to Grieg tells us that three (unspecified) pieces for string orchestra were also completed during this particularly productive period. These pieces seem not to have survived, since none of Delius's known works from this period was composed for string orchestra. The unfinished *Rhapsodic Variations* for large orchestra are dated St-Malo, September 1888; and the *Suite* for violin and orchestra was probably also written at St-Malo. Never before had he produced so much as now. He hoped—ever optimistically—to get the string pieces performed in Paris, and had somehow been led to believe that his *Florida* suite would be given in London in the winter by the conductor August Manns. In the event, neither of these expectations, like so many others during the next decade, were to be fulfilled.

The only cloud on the sunny horizon of St-Malo was the problem of his future base. He would certainly return to the rue Cambon late in October. He now decided that, all in all, he liked France: he was composing successfully, on his own terms at least, and the inconveniences of Paris were, it seemed, forgotten. There were concerts that he wished to attend, including a performance of Beethoven's Ninth Symphony at the Conservatoire to which he looked forward with particular pleasure; and he thought to have found in Paris a poet who was willing to write an operatic libretto for him. On the other hand the idea of going on from Paris and spending the rest of the winter once more in Leipzig was tempting. If only the Griegs could do the same, then there would be no problem, as he had spent so much time with them there the previous winter, establishing a friendship that was equally cherished on either side. However, as time went by in St-Malo, he gradually became reconciled to the idea of wintering in Paris. He was enjoying life and the picture was gilded by the further contentment and fulfilment that the creation of much music was giving him. He began to look forward to his return to Paris with the eagerness and excitement of those early days there a few months earlier. Now was the time to encourage his friends, particularly Grieg, to come and share the thrills and beauties of the city with him. For Delius Paris—"ten times more beautiful than London"—harboured a rich musical and theatrical life, poets, painters, musicians, and not the least an uncle who after all was (in Delius's words) "a splendid fellow". Such were his considerations as the time to leave St-Malo drew closer. Looking still further ahead he felt that the ideal solution would probably be to spend four months of the year in Paris, or maybe even Leipzig, and the remaining eight months in comparative isolation in Norway where he could work quietly. His taste for independence and seclusion was already well developed, and a small place in Norway would suit him perfectly: "Streets and smoke deform our ideas. One must breathe pure air before one can think purely".[1]

18

CHAPTER TWO

Ville d'Avray and Croissy

DELIUS SOON FOUND THE SECLUSION HE WAS SEEKING, for within some three weeks of returning to Paris he had moved from Theodor's apartment to the thickly wooded suburb of Ville d'Avray. This was little more than a village of some 1500 inhabitants, no more than eight or nine miles from the centre of Paris in the direction of Versailles. Until the early nineteenth century the forests in the area had been a favoured royal hunting-ground; then, in the wake of royalty, came the more wealthy bourgeois Parisians who established spring and summer residences there; and of course Corot, whose family home bordered on one of the two small lakes in a wooded area dipping just south of the Versailles road, celebrated Ville d'Avray in his paintings around the middle of the century. Delius rented a little two-roomed cottage, the *Chalet des Lilas, à la Chaumière,* standing "quite alone on the bank of a small lake in a wood", as he soon wrote to Grieg. Close by was a small restaurant where he could take his meals. He could work undisturbed, and it felt to him as if he were a hundred miles from Paris. Yet the Concerts Lamoureux were only a short train-journey away and Delius was indeed soon back in town to hear René Chansarel play Grieg's concerto. Furthermore he was on friendly terms with a nineteen-year-old Norwegian violinist, Arve Arvesen, who was studying in Paris under Marsick. They had probably first made friends in Leipzig a little earlier, and this friendship now rapidly ripened.

Delius was watching General Boulanger's political progress with some interest and perhaps even a little alarm at this time, and felt that a revolution was in the offing: "It will be interesting to participate"—a sentiment echoed by his friend Christian Sinding, who savoured the idea of joining Delius in France and taking part. Delius's interest in current affairs and political events was a fairly lively one, although one feels that the Norwegian political scene interested him more deeply—at any rate during these Paris years. His grasp of Norwegian affairs was a source of surprise and even admiration to more than one of the many friends he was making in that country. Norway too, he felt, was in need of a revolution—one that would sever that country's unhappy links with Sweden. Allied with the distrust that Delius felt for politicians was a sympathy for anarchists and some of their causes—something that people who only know his patrician style of later years may find surprising.

By November he had completed a string quartet. Only the latter portion of the work remains to us, but we do know that Sinding, still in Leipzig, to whom he straightway sent it in the hope that his friend could persuade the Brodsky Quartet to perform it, thought that it looked "damned good". "You are indeed a real devil for work", he wrote. "In addition to all you've already done this year—another quartet for strings".

Christmas and the New Year were spent at Theodor's. For all the advantages of the little Chalet des Lilas, it tended, as Delius found to his cost, to get rather damp in the winter. He took a heavy cold with him to Paris and this lingered on, delaying him in his intention to start on a new work at the beginning of the year. Returning to Ville d'Avray he particularly enjoyed a weekend visit at the beginning of February by his friend Arvesen in the company of a painter, also from Norway, Eyolf Soot. Soot may already have known the area, since he had spent the first of several winters in France studying on a scholarship in Paris back in 1885, when he had travelled down from Norway with Edvard Munch. *A Landscape near St Cloud* by him dates from 1889. Delius and Arvesen made music together, playing the Grieg C Minor Sonata, and all three took a midnight walk in the woods, which looked extraordinarily beautiful under a hard frost and moonlight. A few days later he was back at the rue Cambon, determined finally to get rid of the persistent cold which was undermining his otherwise pleasurable stay at Ville d'Avray. He amused himself by sketching entr'acte music (no longer extant) for *Emperor and Galilean* by Ibsen, a writer whose works he read avidly. Grieg decided that his friend's debility must be due to overwork: "Or it may even be: 'Où est la femme?'!" He recommended gymnastics regularly each morning as a sure antidote to Delius's troubles, and himself caused Sinding no small alarm by telling him that Delius had gone to Paris on account of his health. Sinding had already begun to worry about Delius, for his friend, normally regular in his correspondence, had not answered his last two letters.

An uncertainly dated letter from the artist Charles Boutet de Monvel, in Nice, was probably written to Delius in February 1889: "Poor you, with your severe cold spells and here we take our coffee on

20

Ville d'Avray: Corot's lake

the terrace and bask in the warm sunshine". Boutet, then thirty-five, was trying to establish himself in Nice as a portrait painter to the wealthy Anglo-American colony. He had a weakness for the gaming-table together with that ingenuous belief in an ultimate system to beat the bank that is the hallmark of the born gambler. He was replying to a letter from Delius, his "dear, dear friend", which had much affected him: he knew Delius's "kindness of heart" only too well. His imagination conjured up an idealised world for the two of them to share: ". . . we'll buy an old carriage and we'll drift around the world—We'll take along our best clothes to go to the receptions the Préfêts on our route will give for us. And ever on to the land of our dreams, where cares are unknown, where the women are beautiful and where there is inspiration for our genius!" Something of his picaresque view of life was undoubtedly shared by Delius: he had the Romantic dream shared by many a young artist of setting out on a sunlit highroad, voyaging, creating, loving, without obvious end. His long excursions over the Norwegian mountains were the closest he came to realising this ideal, which was indeed shared by at least one other friend, Halfdan Jebe. This Rabelaisian Norwegian, a virtuoso violinist, we find just a few years later constantly exhorting Delius to put everything else aside and join him on an endless safari round the world whose main ingredients were to be wine, women and song.

By March Delius, fully recovered, was back in Yorkshire on a visit to his family. He met Grieg once again and together the two men discussed plans for a summer holiday tour in Norway. One disappointment Delius met with this month, however, took the form of a letter from August Manns in which the conductor declined to perform *Florida,* though hinting that he might be able to find more time for it at a later date. The month of April was particularly warm and beautiful and Delius seldom felt tempted to leave Ville d'Avray for the city. In two months' time he was to set off for his holiday with Grieg; Sinding too was to come, and correspondence between the three men now centred on the walking tour they were to undertake in the Jotunheim mountains. Arvesen probably came out on occasion to Ville d'Avray, as Sinding had suggested to Delius that their young violinist friend should play through the different parts of the string quartet that Sinding had been correcting on Delius's behalf, to see if the composer agreed with his alterations.

By early June, Delius had probably left Ville d'Avray for good, since in a letter to Grieg he now gave the rue Cambon address. There is evidence of a romantic relationship about this time, hinted at in Grieg's letter to Delius of 1 June: "We had better discuss personally your involvement with the splendid god Eros". Nonetheless, whatever other matters he may have had on hand, musically Delius had been particularly active during the past two months. He had largely

22

completed his *Petite Suite d'Orchestre,* and dissatisfied with the *Florida* suite, had already finished revising two of its movements. (It should perhaps be mentioned that it is only the revision of the third movement that survives and is incorporated in the published version). The first version he now judged clumsy and poorly orchestrated: "Only here have I really learnt what orchestration is". He continued to study Grieg's violin sonata, which he loved and which he was rehearsing with Arvesen, no doubt intending to play it for Grieg in Norway. *Peer Gynt* he was now reading for the fifth time, this time in Norwegian with the help of a dictionary, and by the end of the summer he had established a good working knowledge of the language.

Late in June Delius left Paris on the first stage of the Norwegian tour with Sinding. They travelled by way of Hamar (where for a week they joined Arvesen who was staying at his family home), Christiania and Bergen, before arriving at Troldhaugen, home of the Griegs, in the middle of July. Two more friends from Leipzig days, Busoni and Svendsen, had also intended to come, but Sinding probably dissuaded them when Grieg told him that the party was really becoming too large for the Jotunheim tour.

Returning to Paris in September, Delius once again stayed initially with his uncle, with whom he visited the Paris Exhibition, a colossal cultural hotch-potch which nonetheless offered wells of inspiration to artists of the period. He was already working again at full pressure. Understandably, the prospect of another winter in the damp atmosphere of Ville d'Avray, which he had left in the early summer, had not appealed to him, and he had already found accommodation to suit him better, arranging to rent from 15 October an apartment in a pleasant house at Croissy-sur-Seine, some six miles to the north-west of his former little cottage near the lake. His

8 boulevard de la Mairie, Croissy

predilection for the haunts of painters is already evident, for if Corot had celebrated Ville d'Avray, the Impressionists had only recently been flourishing in and around Croissy, as many views of this and other nearby stretches of the river testify. One of the great attractions of Croissy had been a large floating café-restaurant on the Seine, *La Grenouillère,* immortalised in innumerable Impressionist canvases, but this was totally destroyed in 1889, the year of Delius's arrival in the district, and with it had gone the little town's most popular tourist attraction. Parisians had come in droves to partake of its widely-advertised and brilliantly-illuminated evening spectacles, particularly during the spring and summer, and the hasty erection close by of a Swedish pavilion removed at the end of the Paris Exhibition was no substitute for the deeply-mourned *Grenouillère.* Delius lived in one of Croissy's principal streets: 8 boulevard de la Mairie, almost opposite the Mairie itself. The quiet old house, set back just a little from its neighbours, was not very large—rather long and low—and behind it stretched a pleasant garden. The whole place was an oasis of tranquillity, with much of the atmosphere of a quiet little country town. Once again, soon after his arrival Delius settled down to hard work: we know that he completed his Musset setting, *Chanson de Fortunio,* in November, and he also sketched two piano pieces, *Valse* and *Rêverie,* about this time. His output during the whole of 1889 was not inconsiderable, and fairly varied in scope, but it is not an easy task to range in order of composition his individual works of that year with more accuracy. Apart from those already mentioned, they included *Sakuntala,* a setting of words by the Danish poet Holger Drachmann, for tenor and orchestra; an orchestral piece *Idylle de Printemps;* a *Romance* for violin and piano; and a start on the *Seven Songs from the Norwegian,* completed the following year. Grieg's long-awaited visit to Paris materialised in December and the two men were able to meet again. Delius had, incidentally, just drafted an orchestral arrangement of his friend's *Norwegian Bridal Procession.* His hopes, however, of spending Christmas Eve together with Grieg and his wife, as he had done two years earlier in Leipzig, were not to be realised, for the Griegs had been invited for the occasion to the Paris home of a compatriot novelist, Jonas Lie. On that earlier occasion in 1887, Delius, the Griegs, Sinding and Johan Halvorsen had dined and made music until 2.30 on Christmas morning and, contrary to previous accounts, Delius *had* played to his friends his *Norwegian Sleigh Ride,* as he then called it, in what was probably its original version for piano. [2]

Of Delius's movements during the first three months of 1890 little record remains, but in his own words he spent the winter "working very hard". At the beginning of the year Grieg wrote for him a letter of introduction to Vincent d'Indy, but we do not know if the introduction was effected at the time. The winter was exceptionally cold and an influenza epidemic raged through Paris, where the ice on the Seine was so thick that it had to be dynamited to keep the barges moving. It was fortunate indeed that he no longer lived at Ville d'Avray and that he could now partake of his landlady's excellent and warming *pot au feu* in the house at Croissy. "I have never tasted anything quite so good", he reminisced nostalgically in later years. By the beginning of April the harsh winter seemed at long last to have released its hold. In the garden the fruit trees were in full bloom and the weather had at last decided to be springlike. Delius would take long walks every day and felt "remarkably well and fresh". He began to make plans for the summer and it looked as if his next trip would be to Leipzig in June. His mood this spring is summarised by the shortest of anecdotes: "One evening, a lovely late spring evening, whilst I was walking in the garden enjoying the fine weather the full moon rose above the garden in a cloudless sky. Quite overcome I shouted [to the gardener] to look. He, looking up from his work and scanning the horizon all round, said: "Mais qu'est-ce qu'il y a—je ne vois rien." And I suddenly realized what different worlds we lived in." [3]

By now Delius had made the acquaintance of William Molard, a man who in many respects was to exert a considerable influence on his life—in any case certainly on his activities in Paris during the 1890s. As with many of Delius's early friendships it seems impossible to pinpoint the first meeting and what led to it, but the fact that Molard's mother was Norwegian, that he spoke his mother tongue fluently, that he and the Swedish sculptress Ida Ericson, whom he was to marry in 1891, kept, or were shortly to keep, open house for artists, writers and musicians, and that fellow Scandinavians in particular formed the circle in which he so amiably moved, can lead us reasonably to assume that Delius became acquainted with him through his Scandinavian rather than his French friends. The first evidence of their friendship comes in a letter that Delius wrote to Johan Selmer on 9 April 1890: "Through Molard I have had the opportunity to see one of your scores: *The Spirit of the North.*"

That briefly said, we can leave Molard for the moment, since he and his circle will form the core of this study, but Selmer makes an interesting parenthesis. Born in Christiania in 1844, he was a leading Norwegian composer and like many others of his generation was influenced considerably by Berlioz. He had studied with Ambroise Thomas and others in Paris and had had a fairly chequered career, taking part in the Commune uprising in 1871 and then being obliged to flee Paris for the safety of Norway; it was inevitably some time before he was able to return. He met Delius in Paris in April 1890 and they exchanged some scores, including Selmer's *Scènes Funèbres.*

Delius liked Selmer's work, if he did not particularly take to the man himself, since he told Selmer that he much admired *The Spirit of the North* (a "masterly score") and the two men agreed to meet in Leipzig in the summer. In his turn Selmer asked Delius if he would make a translation into English of his song *Angelus*.

It seems that William Molard intended to accompany Delius on this trip to Leipzig, but no evidence seems to have been left for us to know for sure whether he did or not. Selmer arrived first, late in May, and urged Delius and Molard to arrive in time to join him for *Die Meistersinger* on the 30th. More Wagner was to follow in June. Delius stayed, in fact, in Leipzig for over three weeks (apparently at his former lodgings at Harkortstrasse 5), linking up again with his friend from student days, Christian Sinding. Nina Grieg was delighted that he was back in circulation, writing from Norway: "I have always thought that it was a little too lonely for you in Croissy. I do not know if this was really the case, but some time ago in Paris I very definitely had that impression." In Leipzig Delius paid fifty Marks in order to have the rare chance of rehearsing for $2\frac{1}{2}$ hours some of his orchestral works—we do not, unfortunately, know exactly which—but was angered when Selmer came into the hall and took over the baton, stealing some of his colleague's precious paid-up time for one of his own pieces. Apart from this, Delius was "quite contented" with the rehearsal . . .

The whole of July was spent in Jersey, in spite of exhortations from Norwegian friends such as Grieg and the painter Gudmund Stenersen to join them in the mountains. The summer peregrinations continued till the middle of October; at the end of July he made short trips to Paris, Normandy and Croissy, in that order, and in the middle of August he returned to St-Malo, to the Maison Insley at Sillon, where he had spent his first delightful summer in France two years previously. Grieg lamented that he would have no walking companion in the Jotunheim this summer: "How wonderful it would be if you were to surprise me. It would certainly be very good for you, especially for your nerves, for I'll wager the God of Love is active". To which Delius replied that he would definitely come next summer: "You speak of my nerves. I assure you I haven't any any more. I have never been so fresh and active. The God of Love has been very quiet, never quite absent but, after all, more platonic. I've been bathing almost the whole summer; here in St. Malo it is absolutely marvellous and suits me and my work very well".

As before, a "very busy" winter of 1890-91 was spent at Croissy, with the pattern of excursions to Paris continuing. Much had been achieved in 1890. Works already started that had been completed during the course of the year included the *Seven Songs from the Norwegian,* the *Petite Suite d'Orchestre* and the *Three small tone* poems (*Summer Evening, Winter Night (Sleigh Ride)* and *Spring Morning)*. His *Légendes* (or *Sagen)* for piano and orchestra was to remain unfinished, unlike a *Suite* in three movements for small orchestra, completed that year. The beginnings of *Irmelin,* too, are assumed to date from 1890, although the bulk of the opera was almost certainly written in 1892; also begun were four Heine songs and *Paa Vidderne* (On the Heights), variously termed by Delius 'symphonic poem' or 'overture'. [4]

"I have always admired you for . . . keeping to your main plan without letting yourself be influenced too much by external circumstances", wrote Sinding in the spring, for by March Delius had finished the first version at least of his overture *Paa Vidderne,* and a number of vocal works were in hand. In March came a visit to the family home at Bradford, followed by a few days in London. "All goes well as concerns my spiritual development & my material affairs grieve me little. I have enough to eat and for the present I am satisfied with that." Delius was clearly contented with his life and work.

Sinding was now back in Christiania, and a lively letter he wrote in April to Delius tells of his plan to come to Paris the following winter: "Leipzig and Munich I now know almost too well, and Berlin from my stay there last winter. Berlin seems to me to be smaller and pettier than I had imagined. In spite of its millions of inhabitants, it doesn't make much more of an impression than, say, Leipzig. And gossip flourishes there in the greatest profusion. If somebody farts in the street the whole town knows it at once".

As evidenced from greetings from Selmer as well as Sinding during the first half of 1891, Delius was seeing a good deal of Arve Arvesen. Another Norwegian friendship he forged was with Bergliot Bjørnson, daughter of the poet. She was studying in Paris with Mme Marchesi, the great teacher of singing, and Delius was on sufficiently intimate terms with Bergliot for her to arrange for him to stay with her family for a week during the course of the visit to Norway that he was to make in the summer of 1891. He had set at least five of her father's poems to music between 1885 and 1890, and another was to come: it was in 1890 that Bjørnson had sent his daughter a poem, written long before, which his wife had just found among his papers: *Skogen gir susende, langsom besked.* "Isn't it beautiful?" he wrote to Bergliot. "Someone should set it to music". [5] Bergliot evidently showed the poem to Delius, for he did indeed set the piece soon after.

Early in 1891 we find Paul Gauguin, the painter, in Paris, living for most of the time close by the little crémerie at 13 rue de la Grande Chaumière that was run by the benevolent Madame Charlotte Caron, to the great advantage of many of the more impecunious artists of the quarter. Already discernibly a giant among his fellows, he left in the spring on his first voyage to Tahiti. Boutet de Monvel was friendly with him at this period, and being something of an amateur photographer, he had Gauguin pose for him in February in his own artist's studio in the rue Vandamme. It is conceivable that Delius chanced to meet Gauguin during this time, although his comparative isolation at Croissy might indicate that it was improbable that he had begun to frequent Montparnasse and Madame Charlotte's crémerie. He certainly remained in touch with Boutet, apparently lending him some money, to judge by a letter that the artist sent him early in June, once again from Nice: "How happy I was to receive your telegram, my dear Fritz, not so much for the money it tells me is on the way, but because it shows me the strength of your affection—It is both heartening and comforting to see that one can count on someone in this world."

The summer tour of Norway came, with visits to the Bjørnsons and the Griegs. He wrote out for Bjørnson a few bars of his setting of *Skogen gir susende,* and spent some time with Iver Holter, the conductor, who was to give his *Paa Vidderne* overture in Christiania on 10 October. In the event this was the very first public performance of an orchestral work by Delius and the composer prolonged his stay in Norway in order to be able to attend it.

CHAPTER THREE

Petit Montrouge

WITH HIS DEPARTURE FOR NORWAY, DELIUS HAD GIVEN up the apartment at Croissy. Probably staying briefly at the rue Cambon on his return, he soon moved to an apartment at 33 rue Ducouëdic, in the Petit Montrouge quarter of Paris. Less than two miles south of the Île de la Cité, this was to be his home for the next few years. Jelka Delius has painted a pen-picture of his new home as she first saw it rather more than four years later: "He had persuaded the proprietor to knock two little rooms into one, and this made a pleasant two-windowed apartment containing a grand piano, a red carpet and a square table. Next it was a tiny bedroom and an equally tiny kitchen. He would rush out, buy a large beefsteak, some eggs and a bunch of watercress. We then put the kettle on the sitting-room fire and lit the oven, a charcoal affair in the kitchen where, as always, he did his own cooking, something he had learnt during his Florida days".[6] Just why for the only time in his life Delius chose to live near the heart of a city the size of Paris is not clear. One thing is certain: women found him attractive, and intimate relationships were to be a salient feature of his years in Paris. Nina Grieg, surprised to have had no word from him by the middle of November, suspected that a love affair was preoccupying him. Delius, on the other hand, attempted to assure her that affairs were a habit he hoped to break. Nina found this difficult to accept—nor was she willing to commend the idea of total abstinence. But she was still mystified as to Delius's move: "I do not really understand, at least as far as I know you, how you can live in Paris and not in the country. Do you not long for trees and fields, for quiet paths, where no-one walks?" Whatever the case, at least cultural life in Paris was now immediately accessible to him, and friends could be entertained without railway timetables having to be consulted. He went to hear a "remarkable" performance by Colonne

29

of Beethoven's Ninth Symphony and the Bacchanale from *Tannhäuser;* and a first hearing of Strauss's *Don Juan,* given by Lamoureux, greatly interested him. He could now look back with some satisfaction on the completion of a year's work characterised by its emphasis on vocal pieces: these included the *Four songs to words by Heine, Three English songs* (Shelley), *Lyse Naetter* (Drachmann), and the song cycle for tenor and orchestra *Maud,* a setting of five of Tennyson's poems.

In February 1892 he was in London for a while, taking the opportunity on the 20th of that month to attend the glittering first night of Wilde's *Lady Windermere's Fan* at the St. James's Theatre. Also present were the rising young English poet Richard Le Gallienne and his wife. Delius had some time in 1891 written to Le Gallienne, suggesting collaboration on an opera; the poet had replied in the politest of terms, thanking Delius for the honour of asking him but regretfully declining: no libretto of his would do justice to Delius's score.[7] Somehow, however, the idea stayed alive, with Le Gallienne finally suggesting the old story of Endymion, which had long been dear to him. In late February 1892 we find Delius staying at the Le Galliennes' home in Hanwell, Middlesex, with the two men hard at work on their project. Norway incidentally was a shared interest, Le Gallienne having visited that country for the first time the previous year. On the 27th Le Gallienne wrote to his mother: "Our Frenchman [sic] left us last night. We liked him much. He is sure to do something. I never saw a man with such irresistible will, and as it is directed with intelligence, he is sure to come to the front. Certainly he deserves to. We have sketched out the plot of a little opera together on the story of Endymion—and he has gone back full of it. He seems to have the working capacities of a brewer's horse. Would they were mine!"[8]

The beginning of March saw Delius back in Paris. "I am now taken up by a larger work", he wrote to Mrs. Randi Blehr, a Norwegian friend. He wrote too to the Griegs to tell them of his plans (a letter which has not survived), and Nina Grieg replied asking why he should not write a libretto himself. The picture is confused, because the libretto he *did* write was for *Irmelin,* itself completed in 1892, and Nina's later letter of 21 September might refer either to *Irmelin* or to the ill-starred 'Endymion': "Aha! So you have had bad luck with your opera, you poor fellow. You once wrote to me of an English poet with whom you agreed. What has happened to him?" A letter from Sinding, too, in October, implies that Delius had by now been let down by an intended librettist. At all events, we hear no more of the Delius—Le Gallienne collaboration, and no musical sketches specifically identifiable as relating to 'Endymion' remain. Beecham's reminder to us—that around this time Delius destroyed a considerable amount of music that he had composed—takes on extra point.

Sinding was in Paris now, greatly enjoying his stay there, according to Delius, who introduced him to Molard and Boutet de Monvel. The city was again in the grip of yet another particularly cold winter and Delius could not wait for it to come to an end: ". . . it's only in spring and summer that I really live". The summer in fact was once more spent on the Breton coast. For much of the time he was apparently based as before at St-Malo, and his excursions took him at least as far as Finistère. One can surmise that he pressed on with *Irmelin,* for the work was finished by the end of the year.

During the autumn of 1892 Delius became acquainted with Isidore de Lara, composer, singer and social butterfly *par excellence.* They met at the house of Hope Temple, later—in 1896—to become André Messager's second wife. De Lara found Delius to be "ascetic and unworldly", but took greatly to him: "You have a devoted friend", wrote Emma Calvé to Delius a little later, "who appreciates and believes in you." De Lara was to see a good deal of Delius in Paris, often dining with him at the rue Ducouëdic "on a couple of eggs" (Delius, as we have seen, being in the habit of cooking his own meals). De Lara judged his friend's means to be very small, but the likelihood was that his own intensive cultivation of upper class society in Paris blinkered him to more everyday standards of social intercourse. Delius was certainly able still to live fairly comfortably within the allowances made to him by his family. At all events de Lara seems to have opened the door for his friend to make a foray into the world of the *Almanach de Gotha.* Soon Delius was dining at the home of his new-found mentor in the company of the American-born Princesse Brancaccia and other notables from the upper reaches of Parisian society.

Christmas was spent in Paris with Arvesen, but that is all we know of Delius's movements at the turn of the year. A single and not unexpected clue, however, to his usual winter preoccupation is again furnished by a letter-this time to a Norwegian friend on 4 February 1893: "Recently I have been very busy with my work and I still am". He had certainly finished *Irmelin,* together with the revision of *Paa Vidderne,* by the end of 1892, and had written a Sonata in B for violin and piano. One of the particularly interesting characteristics of these early Paris years was the emphasis on works composed either for violin or voice. Delius's best chances of performance were after all in the salons of the kind promoted by and flourishing in the musical circles into which his uncle had initially introduced him, and in due course he got to know a number of useful singers: Calvé, Georgette Leblanc, Bélina-Lalutinskaja and others. His own preferred instrument was the violin, and one of his closest friends, Arve

Arvesen, was a violinist of great talent who was later to form a celebrated quartet in his native country. Private performances of works of a vocal or instrumental nature were therefore the best that Delius could hope for at present and his output during these years is characterised accordingly.

The general picture of the composer's life at this time, then, is a fairly unusual one. An Englishman in Paris moving by preference among Norwegians or among those generally with close Scandinavian connections. Little to suggest that many really close contacts had yet been made with French artists. Among his principal confidants are the Griegs and Sinding in Norway and Arvesen and Molard in Paris. Only of the Arvesen friendship has scarcely any documentation come down to us;[9] but many of the letters between the Griegs and Delius have been preserved (although not, it seems, a number where Delius discusses with his friends his *affaires de coeur* in any detail) and these form the principal documentary source of Delius's life so far in Paris. Nina Grieg displayed, as we have seen, a lively interest in Delius's relations with the opposite sex, and they even invented an innocent private code in their letters: "to rattle" meant to have a relationship, and "rattlesnake" indicated the object of affection. Odd, but innocuous. Certainly it is not too easy quite to understand what kept Delius in Paris during this initial period, if not a romantic attachment. Until now he had worked hard and on the whole lived quietly since settling in France. Everything points to this—the volume of his output, the letters that have survived, the testimony of his friends. For the next two years or so he was to produce comparatively less, for reasons that will be obvious and acceptable. He was to find himself almost suddenly in a circle of superbly creative, extraordinary and sometimes eccentric people, whose art and experience were to enrich his own.

He suffered another bout of ill-health, probably nothing very serious, around the end of the winter, but soon found time to write a word or two of advice on gambling to Christian Sinding, who tried his luck at Monte-Carlo in the spring. Delius himself stayed in Paris until late June, cherishing hopes that he might somewhere get the recently-completed *Irmelin* performed. A new friend appeared on the scene about now in the form of Harold Bauer, aged just twenty. Bauer had at first trained in his native America to be a violinist, but his more natural bent proved to be for the piano, to which on Paderewski's advice in 1892 he henceforth devoted himself. He arrived in Paris in the spring of 1893 and before long was introduced to Delius by Montague Chester. His comments on Delius, who lived not far from his own lodgings, are of interest: 'I did not care very much for the compositions he showed me, for I found them loose in construction and deficient in contrapuntal writing. We discussed these things very frankly, and he criticized my attitude as being unduly academic, saying that he was not interested in writing in the style of the ancients. This did not mean that he disliked the music of any one of the great composers; on the contrary, his tastes in art were as wide and liberal as could be imagined; but he had the strongest feeling that the first duty of any artist was to find ways in which his own personality could be expressed, whether or not the process conformed to traditional methods. "An artist", said Delius, "will finally be judged by that and nothing else. He must have"—here he hesitated and finally found the expression of his thought in French—"une note à lui".'[10]

Bauer and Delius talked together of many things besides music, and Bauer enjoyed the company of his friend, finding in him "a highly intelligent and original thinker". It was apparently in the apartment that Bauer shared in 1893 with his fellow-musician Serge Achille Rivarde—a New Yorker by birth—that Delius had an opportunity to hear his Violin Sonata in B (which was never published) played. For his part Delius was soon urging de Lara to try to secure an engagement at Monte-Carlo for Bauer, something which de Lara, for all his vague promises to help, never effected.

One other composition dating from 1893, the song *Nuages,* is of interest in that it represents Delius's only setting of words by Jean Richepin, a contemporary poet whom he could possibly have met. In spite of electing to live in France for the major part of his life, Delius showed remarkably little inclination to use French texts as a basis for vocal composition. Musset in 1889 and now Richepin were, it seems, the only French poets apart from Verlaine that he chose to set. His Verlaine songs were *Il pleure dans mon coeur* and *Le ciel est, par-dessus le toit,* both written in 1895, *La lune blanche* (1910), *Chanson d'automne* (1911) and *Avant que tu ne t'en ailles* (1919, completed in 1932). The only other work written to a French text was the one-act lyric drama *Margot la Rouge,* whose libretto was by 'Rosenval'. This work was composed in 1902 specifically for a melodrama competition sponsored by the Italian music publisher Edoardo Sonzogno. Delius never thought much of it, but towards the end of his life salvaged some of the music with the help of Eric Fenby and used it in his *Idyll,* a work which has much of the flavour and atmosphere of the 1899 *Paris.*

It was probably during the spring of 1893, in de Lara's social circles, that Delius developed an interest in occultism (even if, according to his sister, he maintained a healthy scepticism generally on the subject of psychic phenomena). He was just one of many. Occultism was very much a craze of the period. Curtains were being drawn, candles lit and hands laid on tables across the length and breadth of Paris. The courses of the stars were studied, bumps were felt, heads and hands analyzed, cards consulted, to the general excitement of a large section of society. In May de Lara sent an urgent message to Delius: "The Princesse Brancaccia is in a great state of anxiety about her horoscope". Could Delius come and read it for her at 2 o'clock the same day? Another of de Lara's friends and associates was the soprano Emma Calvé, 'a lovely dark woman, with large lustrous eyes, resembling the Italian more than the French type of beauty'.[11] He had first met her in London in 1892 and his *Amy Robsart* was written for her, enjoying for a time a fair success that Delius must have envied. The role with which she became most closely identified, however, was that of Carmen, which she was to sing all over the world. De Lara introduced Delius to her some time during the first half of 1893 and Delius agreed to cast her horoscope too. The occultist merry-go-round itself continued for some years, although it was not long before Delius got off. Calvé records a dinner party in 1898 at the home of Camille Flammarion: Papus was among the guests, a young lady was hypnotised, and there were "very interesting conversations on astronomy, hypnotism, spiritualism, telepathy, etc."[12]

The summer of 1893 was spent in Norway again. Delius left Paris late in June and established himself at Drøbak, not far from Christiania, sharing a little cottage with Sinding, and visiting friends nearby. By late September he was back in Paris and the social life resumed its course: we find a marquise inviting him to a dinner party; he met the great Papus, acknowledged leader of the occult movement in Paris; and he and Papus received a piquantly phrased invitation from Emma Calvé to dine at her home in the rue Marbeuf: "Nous serons tout à fait entre nous! Deux ou trois occultistes tous braves gens bien simples . . ." Delius in his turn gave a *dîner Bohémien,* and Calvé figured among his guests, as did another of the Papus circle, the Princesse de Lanskoy, Mlle de Wolska, described by one writer as the "deaconess of occultism".[13]

The acquaintanceship with the somewhat younger Papus, whose real name was Dr. Gérard Encausse, resulted in a collaboration which produced a 24-page booklet, published in Paris by Chamuel later the following year, entitled *Anatomie et Physiologie de l'Orchestre,* authorship attributed jointly to Papus and Delius. One doubts if there is very much of Delius in this. Papus must have been one of the most prolific writers who ever lived and his huge treatises on the occult sciences have run to many editions and figure prominently in Paris bookshops even today. They are classics of their genre. Scientific and medical papers flowed from his pen too. He was to hold all kinds of honorary positions and offices and to become President of the Syndicat de l'Occultisme. A genial bear of a man, with a ruddy face and a shaggy black beard, he must have cut an original figure in Parisian society, where he was much in demand.

Not surprisingly Strindberg and he were soon introduced (could this even have been through Delius's agency?) when the former came to Paris. More than probably his acquaintanceship with Delius gave him the opportunity to discuss and develop theories which had already buzzed through his fertile brain, and it was Delius's part to set out for him the composition of the orchestra and generally to lend a

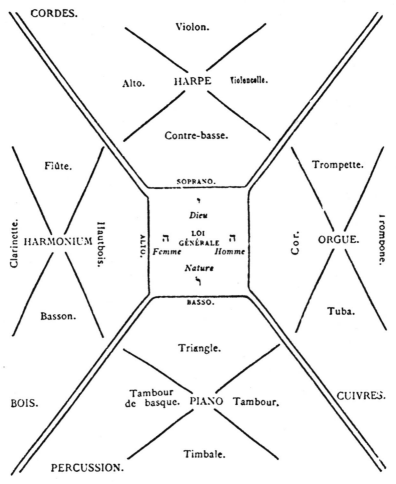

A page from 'Anatomie et Physiologie de l'Orchestre

helping hand. "A Cabalist and a Musician", ran a blurb for the booklet, "have come together to publish this original thought: the orchestra is analogous to a living being composed of a body, a doubly-polarised soul and a mind".[14] Or as one reviewer put it: "Papus and Delins [sic] endeavour to find a new orchestral system, with the aid, moreover, of the . . . Cabala".[15] Although in the work the authors affirmed that the *Anatomie* was merely a prelude to a much more considerable treatise (which was to bear the title *Traité systématique d'Orchestre)*, they took the precaution to point out that this would only follow 'if the authors feel it will interest the musical world'. In fact it appears that the larger book was already under way, but the dull thud which this curious monograph must have produced when dropped at the feet of 'the musical world' probably convinced Papus and Delius that whatever passing interest it may have held for occultist circles, the practising musician was simply not interested—and they therefore abandoned their larger project. In due course Delius sent a copy of the *Anatomie* to his friend from student days in Leipzig, the Hungarian composer Ottokar Nováček. The latter was no doubt grateful for the thought, but probably shared the opinion of other of Delius's friends when he wrote: "I personally feel myself to be a stranger to your views". Papus, incidentally, had the good sense to practise his beliefs from beyond the grave. Gauguin's dealer, Ambroise Vollard, once told of hearing how, at the home of one of their mutual acquaintances, Papus, some time after his death in 1916, had 'manifested his presence' in a useful and salutary fashion.[16]

1893 had, so far as we know, yielded little in compositional terms: a string quartet and the Richepin song are about all that we can accurately assign to that year. But then, early in 1894, de Lara's string-pulling succeeded in bringing about a real morale-booster—a full-scale performance of an orchestral work by Delius in Monte-Carlo.[17] Theodor Delius had, it seems, weighed in with a subvention, and *Paa Vidderne,* now reworked and dubbed *Sur les cimes,* was given at the seventh international concert of the season, which was consecrated entirely to British music. Balfe's *Bohemian Girl* overture opened the programme, and this was followed by works by Mackenzie, M. [?] Oakeley, Sullivan, Parish Alvars, Godfrey, "and finally, a symphonic poem, *Sur les cimes* (1st performance) [sic] by Delius, which was particularly noticed by true musicians and in which the orchestra of M Steck wrought wonders". The correspondent of *Le Figaro,* where this review appeared on Friday 2 March, restricted himself to just this critical comment on the whole "rich programme", so Delius did particularly well by him. But there was praise from another quarter too. De Lara had presented Delius to Princess Alice of Monaco, who attended the concert, and she wrote the following day to tell Delius that she thought it was "splendid music". She had the discernment to add: "I would be very much surprised if you don't attain "Les Cimes" of glory—for you have great science coupled to great art". She furthermore offered to get some more of Delius's compositions performed in Monte-Carlo if he would send his next completed work to her. Nothing, however, seems to have come of this.

Papus

Theodor Delius

13 rue de la Grande Chaumière: Madame Charlotte at the window above her crémerie (panel by Mucha to the left, by Slewinski to the right)

A Gauguin 'at home' in the artist's studio at 6 rue Vercingétorix. Standing, left and centre, Paul Sérusier and Gauguin's mistress, Annah 'the Javanese'

Ida in the Molards' studio at 6 rue Vercingétorix

Portrait of Molard by Gauguin

Julien Leclercq

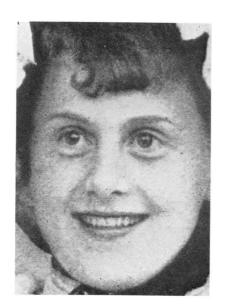

Bergliot Bjørnson

Portrait of Slewinski (detail)
by Gauguin

41

overleaf: 'A Fritz Delius: souvenir d'amitié & de vive sympathie—G. Daniel de Monfreid, Fév. 93'

*No. 6, rue Vercingétorix: showing the studios of Paul Gauguin
(above) and William and Ida Molard (below)*

Jacques Arsène Coulangheon: woodcut 'after Judith' by P-E. Vibert

Isidore de Lara

Alphonse Mucha

Georges-Daniel de Monfreid:
Self-portrait

Jean Richepin

CHAPTER FOUR

The Molard Circle

BY NOW—THAT IS, THE END OF FEBRUARY 1894—DELIUS was more clearly moving into another phase of his life in Paris, for a fresh circle, genuinely Bohemian in its life-style and as such affording an acute contrast to the de Lara social set, had opened to take him in. Gauguin had returned to France the previous August, and soon made his way back to his old stamping-ground in Montparnasse, the rue de la Grande Chaumière, where the Académie Colarossi, a noted art school, faced Madame Charlotte's crémerie. He moved into No. 8—next door to the Academy—where a then little-known Czech painter, Alphonse Mucha, had offered him the use of his studio. The first quarter's rent he paid in advance with money borrowed from Charlotte. Mucha was in the habit of taking his meals at the crémerie, as was another painter friend of Gauguin, Georges-Daniel de Monfreid. Yet another habitué was the Polish painter, Wladyslaw Slewinski, who had initially studied at the Colarossi and had known Gauguin well for some five or six years. Charlotte's clientèle was a genuinely international one and many of her 'students' were, like Gauguin, well into middle age. The crémerie, as Delius remembered it, was 'a little place of the utmost simplicity, where hardly ten people could sit down at a time and where one's meal generally cost one franc, or a franc-fifty including coffee'.

Gauguin, settling down for the time being, was soon painting, starting work too on his book *Noa-Noa*. Then around the beginning of 1894 he moved into new lodgings at 6 rue Vercingétorix belonging to his rue de la Grande Chaumière landlord. His friend Daniel de Monfreid accompanied him up the wooden staircase leading from the courtyard on the day he moved in. Close by were two Montparnasse landmarks: the railway station and, a block or two to the west, the vast Cimetière de Montparnasse. Gauguin quickly made friends with the couple living below, William and Ida Molard, and the extraordinary 'at homes' at the rue Vercingétorix were soon under way. Delius, then, possibly met Gauguin for the first time during the early days of 1894 at the Molards', and it was probably about then, too, that he began to frequent Charlotte's crémerie, in order to meet and talk with Gauguin and some of his friends. However, he did know Daniel de Monfreid as early as February 1893 (perhaps through Boutet de Monvel), since this is the date that Monfreid's pastel study of the composer bears, and one cannot discount the possibility that Delius already then was taking the occasional meal *chez Charlotte.*

It is worth looking at some of these people in greater detail, since many were on good terms with Delius at this period, and just a few of his Montparnasse friendships were to last a score of years or more. One or two of the principal figures, such as Gauguin and Mucha, are fairly well documented today; some other bright stars of the time have, however, faded into almost complete obscurity.

Gauguin, now at the age of 45, was very much a focus of attention in this circle. A contemporary journalist leaves a pen-picture of him: "Gauguin is built like a Hercules: his greying hair is curly, his features are energetic, his eyes clear; and when he smiles in his characteristic way he seems alike gentle, shy, and ironical".[18] Like Delius, Gauguin had an unshakeable belief in his own creative

Portrait of Gauguin
by Judith Ericson Molard

genius and ability. Already acknowledged as the leading Symbolist painter of the day he was supremely confident of his place in the pantheon of great artists: "He never thinks", wrote his abandoned wife, "of anything but himself and his own convenience, and is full of self-satisfied admiration of his own greatness."[19] As an artist he considered himself an aristocrat, and in his search for sublimity, beauty, taste and good manners—all qualities which he admired intensely—he was prepared to ride rough-shod over men he considered petty and talentless: "There's nothing to be gained by trying to ingratiate oneself with idiots—and I have reason for despising a large proportion of humanity".[20]

Like Delius, too, Gauguin sought a form of isolation which both stimulated and allowed time for reflection—he recreated from memory rather than from the model: "Have a model", was his advice to the young artist, but while painting "draw the curtain over it".[21]

On this count he particularly admired Beethoven as an artist: "Beethoven was blind [sic] and deaf, he was isolated from everything, so his works are redolent of the artist living in a world of his own"[22]—which draws us to his attitude to music: even if he largely abjured the 'rules' of the Symbolists, Gauguin certainly shared one of their principal views: that the various arts were closely related and that artists working in various fields could express the same ideas, emotions and moods. Music always fascinated him, even though he confessed himself musically to be "a Philistine". He turned to his guitar as a favourite form of relaxation both during these rue Vercingétorix days and after, and he had, too, a piano in his studio, liking to tackle the easier classical pieces. It was to Molard that he confessed: "I have always had a mania for relating painting to music, which, since I cannot understand it scientifically, becomes a little more comprehensible to me through the relationship I discern between these two arts".[23] Yet another of Delius's friends, Edvard Munch, also acknowledged a rapport between painting and music, and could even talk about his own paintings as "musical notes".

Consider Delius and his music in the light of the theories and indeed the works of his painter friends. Who would find it difficult to see Gauguin's characteristic techniques—vigorous brushwork, bold colouring and exotic subject matter—in *Koanga,* a work begun in 1895, the year when the painter finally took his leave of Paris? Similarly, it would be idle to credit coincidence alone with a series of inter-related inspirations of both Delius and Munch, from *A Mass of Life* and its progenitive *Mitternachtslied Zarathustras* (1899), through to a work saturated in the melancholia that typifies Munch, *Fennimore and Gerda,* in 1909. The cover illustration to the vocal score of *Fennimore,* as published in 1919, is indeed a pastiche of Munch, and one remembers that the artist had at one time discussed with Delius the possibility of a joint creative synthesis which would also comprise a literary element: the work of Jens Peter Jacobsen. The Impressionists on the other hand had been around for longer than Gauguin and Munch, and Delius's earliest orchestral work, the *Florida* suite (1887), had already taken the form of a series of impressionistic pictures of the St Johns River and its borders, remembered from two years earlier (he had drawn the curtain over the model...). But the peak of Delius's technical ability was reached at a time when he had at last found both the setting and the calmness of mind in which to achieve a perfect synthesis of Impressionism. This was around 1911, when *Summer Night on the River* was composed, shortly after the revision of *In a Summer Garden.* Both works were created in the tranquil and shimmering beauty that the river Loing and its banks of trees and meadows bestowed upon Delius's home village of Grez, and both works were imbued with the *pointilliste* techniques that his wife Jelka employed in the light and airy canvases that she herself was executing with consummate talent during these years of joint artistic fulfilment.

Gauguin's most trusted and devoted friend, the gentle and grave-faced Daniel de Monfreid was, at the age now of almost 38, some six years older than Delius. He was a tall, bearded man, with a loping gait and a character that was serene and sympathetic. He had first met Gauguin about 1887 at the home of a mutual painter friend, Emile Schuffenecker. Monfreid was a particularly close friend of Aristide Maillol, the young sculptor, whom he introduced to Delius. He had resources which enabled him comfortably to maintain both a wife and a yacht, and his friends dubbed him "The Captain". He painted with talent but had the innate modesty to accept that his own gifts were inferior to those of a number of his companions—with the result that he spent much of his life helping his friends, most notably Gauguin and Maillol, to sell their works and to arrange exhibitions, sustaining them in countless smaller ways. He did not sell his own works; those which he did not keep he gave away. "I have endeavoured to paint simply and well", he was to write to Gauguin.[24] "As long as after my death people find a few good things of mine and judge them worth keeping . . ."[25] Little wonder that Delius took greatly to this essentially good man, in whom, to use Gauguin's own words, he must have found "une belle nature d'homme et d'artiste".[26]

Wladyslaw Slewinski was some eight years older than Delius. He had arrived in Paris in 1888, escaping from family difficulties and debts in his native Poland and registering, as Gauguin and Monfreid had done in their time, as a student at the Académie Colarossi. He soon grew to admire Gauguin greatly, was with him in Brittany quite often, and his painting, only begun seriously in France, was much influenced by Gauguin and others of the Pont-Aven group. Together with Monfreid, Slewinski was to remain almost the only one of his friends whom Gauguin trusted implicitly, describing him in a letter to Molard as "a perfect gentleman".[27] Gauguin painted a portrait of Slewinski, just as he did of Molard around this time.[28]

Slewinski was on particularly good terms with Mucha, another well-liked student at the Colarossi, and in fact three or four years earlier had originally found the impoverished Czech painter his first room (he was to move to others) in the rue de la Grande Chaumière, immediately above the crémerie. Living as he did in the house itself, Mucha became, according to the account of his son, "a sort of patron to a continually changing crowd: it was he and Slewinski who usually took charge of new arrivals and introduced them to the others. At the entrance to the crémerie stood two resplendent boards for the greater glory of the establishment, the one with a floral theme painted by Slewinski and the other of fruit by Mucha".[29] To think of the

48

paintings by Gauguin, Mucha, Slewinski and others that adorned the little restaurant! By the middle of the 1890s one has the impression that Mucha, basically a serious, dedicated man, was moving away from the others. His Sarah Bernhardt posters, the first of which appeared on the Parisian streets on the 1 January 1895, lifted him to almost overnight celebrity, and he was to move from the rue de la Grande Chaumière in the summer of 1896.

Then there was the Irish painter Roderic O'Conor. An intimate of Gauguin, he had lived in Paris for about nine years now, although like many of the others he generally spent his summers in Brittany. Gauguin liked him much and tried to persuade him to accompany him to the South Seas, but O'Conor declined, sensibly realising the incompatibility of their respective temperaments. It seems quite possible that he met Delius, especially in view of the fact that he was later to paint in and around Grez-sur-Loing, where Delius ultimately settled.

Edvard Munch was not to come into the circle for another year or two, and we do not know how his introduction to Delius came about. Quite possibly though this was through the agency of his Norwegian poet friend Vilhelm Krag, whom Sinding had in 1893 first presented to Delius by means of a letter of introduction. Like Sinding, Grieg set a considerable number of Krag's poems to music and he and his wife sent Delius a book of the young poet's works for Christmas 1891. For his part Delius set just one piece, *Jeg havde en nyskaaren Seljefløjte* more probably around 1893 rather than in 1891, as hitherto thought. It is reasonable to suppose that Delius introduced Krag into the Molard circle, as he certainly did with Munch, who in later life was never to forget how kind the Molards had been to him in Paris at this time.

It was with artists like Gauguin, Munch, Monfreid, Slewinski, Mucha, and Boutet de Monvel that Delius was most at home in Montparnasse and Montrouge. His taste for modern painting and sculpture was developing rapidly and he was soon collecting works by his friends and others. At a time when Rodin's masterpiece *Balzac,* towards the turn of the century, was attracting almost universal odium, Delius was among its few really fervent admirers, and when, in 1901, Rodin came to spend two days at his home in Grez, Delius was overwhelmed with delight—as indeed was his future wife Jelka Rosen (yet another painter)...

Particularly prominent among the writers who frequented the rue de la Grande Chaumière and the rue Vercingétorix at this period was a poet named Julien Leclercq, at the age of 28 one of the younger members of the circle immediately around Gauguin. As yet his only claim to fame was a little volume of poems, *Strophes d'amant,* published in 1891. The contents were mediocre, all pieces written during his early twenties, but if the poetry itself was poor, at least Leclercq *looked* like a poet, slim, with dark curly hair and burning eyes. He had already become acquainted with Gauguin by 1891 and frequented Symbolist circles at this period. He wrote much, but not all of his work was published. Novels, plays, poems, essays, reviews flowed from his pen during the course of his relatively brief life (he died in 1901 at the age of 36), and he produced two books in the mid-nineties in which he analyzed the characters of prominent contemporaries through the study of physiognomy and palmistry. Among his subjects were the Griegs, Ibsen, Rodin, Strindberg, Verlaine, Richepin, Calvé and Maeterlinck. A lengthy essay he wrote on Gauguin, *La lutte pour les peintres,* was published in November 1894 in the *Mercure de France*. He certainly needed the money that he earned from these publications, being even poorer than most of his indigent acquaintances. "Sell the manuscript at any price you can", he had written to a friend in January 1893, ". . . I absolutely need the money".[30]

On one occasion while Strindberg was in Paris, Leclercq joined Delius in playing a trick on the distinguished visitor. Delius invited them both to the rue Ducouëdic for a séance, and there in the darkened room Leclercq asked Delius's table, which was pregnant with spiritual information, what message it had for them. The table began to rap out its message in letters, the first of which was M, but neither Strindberg's eager anticipation nor his minimal sense of humour was finally appeased when the word MERDE at last emerged. "I do not think he ever quite forgave us for this", was Delius's comment.

Leclercq was on the whole not particularly liked by his fellows, who generally regarded him as rather a schemer, even if he did have an ingratiating charm. He was something of a sponger too, staying rent-free in Gauguin's studio when the artist left for Brittany in the summer of 1894 and borrowing money from friends which he showed a marked reluctance to return. The young Judith Ericson-Molard, William's step-daughter, loathed Leclercq, no doubt with something of the jealousy she had for all those who were closer to her hero Gauguin than she could ever hope to be. "He spoke a great deal with the supreme incompetence and marvellous intuition that for him took the place of erudition." With one love-affair just come to an end Leclercq turned his attentions to the precocious Judith: "You don't know what love is", he told her. "All the same, it's not you who'll teach me", came the reply. "Why not me?" "And *why* you, may I ask?" "Because I love you. I've wept all night". "Weep on", retorted Judith, "you'll piss less!" She later remembered restraining herself from throwing insults about his "fetid breath and bad teeth" at him, and for a while—until they stopped arriving—she cheerfully threw away his letters without opening them.

An epilogue to Leclercq: thirty years after his death a *Comité Julien Leclercq* was formed in Armentières to honour this son of the town. Leclercq's former friend and mentor Gabriel Randon, better known under his pen name Jehan Rictus, accepted the honorary presidency, and the elderly Will Molard was invited to become a vice-president.[31]

William Molard

One of the younger writers Delius was occasionally to see at the Molards was Jacques Arsène Coulangheon. Around the turn of the century he began to enjoy a degree of success, publishing two novels and a volume of short stories before suffering an agonising death, from tuberculosis, in the spring of 1904 at the early age of 29. Instead of a hoped-for visit then to the Deliuses at Grez, the Molards, fearfully saddened, attended their young friend's funeral.

Then there was Strindberg, the literary lion of the circle into which he stepped in the summer of 1894. "Paris is a ripe plum just waiting to be picked, and the next season is mine," he had written to a friend in the spring.[32] It was fairly natural that once in Paris he should soon gravitate to the Molard circle, with its strong Scandinavian emphasis, for they had mutual friends and he had known Ida Molard some years earlier in Stockholm. The Scandinavian literary and cultural influence in Paris had just about reached its zenith by the mid-nineties, with Strindberg, Ibsen, Bjørnson, Grieg and others enjoying an extraordinary vogue, which brought in its wake hordes of younger and inevitably less-talented artists and students from the north to the French capital and to which an inevitable reaction set in. Strindberg arrived on 18 August 1894 and the première of his play *The Father* the following December was one of the theatrical events of the season. We know that Gauguin and Rodin were among the first-night audience, and it is perhaps not unreasonable to suppose that others of the Molard circle may have been present. Strindberg had quite recently tried his hand at painting. There seemed after all to be no branch of the arts—or indeed the sciences for that matter—at which he did *not* try his hand; and this was one of the occupations he resumed in Paris, when he even managed to sell some canvases at reasonable prices. He also pursued his work on a host of scientific experiments, prominent among which were his attempts to manufacture pure gold. He soon became a frequent visitor to the Molards, who like Gauguin held regular 'at homes' which seemed to be more or less open to all and sundry. But life in the big city had made him tired and nervous. He wrote to his wife shortly after his arrival in Paris: "here . . . you will be cheated on every hand. Famous men will gabble at you in restaurants for hours until you are dead beat and bored, instead of your enjoying their good books at home in peace . . ." Soon he was taking long walks through the Luxembourg Gardens and in the Latin Quarter. Delius would be his companion on some occasions, Mucha on others. But he could not find peace for his disordered mind, as his letters to his wife later in the autumn bear witness: "What a miserable existence. I detest crowds, but I cannot live alone. So now I am a prey to boon companions, alcohol, nights out, cabarets, headaches and all other sorts of aches . . . When I am alone in a great city, the tavern alone saves me from suicide; all the better, then, if someone drags me there!" One café he began to frequent was Mère Charlotte's, where Delius sometimes saw and talked with him, and it was in fact this milieu that he depicted in his drama *Crimes and Crimes.* He spent the Christmas of 1894 at the Molards, in spite of the "painful irregularity" which he discerned in the atmosphere there, particularly on Christmas Eve: "We at once sit down to dinner and begin to eat it in tumultuously noisy fashion. The young artists are quite irresponsible. Their speeches and gestures are unrestrained and a tone prevails which is out of place in the family . . . I feel irritated and displeased".[33] Nor were his wife's family particularly pleased when early in 1895 they heard from a journalist in Paris that Strindberg was "frequenting the loose Gauguin and Molard set, alcoholic Bohemia." Around the beginning of February 1895 Strindberg moved to No. 12 rue de la Grande Chaumière, where Mucha had also lived for a while, just opposite the crémerie: 'Once settled into a modest furnished room, I continue my chemical experiments all winter, staying at home until the evening, then going out to eat my dinner at a crémerie where some artists of various nationalities have formed a circle. After dinner I visit the family I once quitted so abruptly during a momentary attack of moral rigour. The whole circle of anarchistic artists meets there, and I feel myself condemned to endure what I have tried to avoid: loose living, lax morals, deliberate godlessness. There is a great deal of talent gathered together there, an infinite amount of wit, one of them [Gauguin] possesses real genius and has won a respected name for himself.'[34] For Leclercq this was the beginning of a period that he was to refer to as 'our great year'.

Strindberg was yet another of the company for whom the ever-observant and malicious Judith had a cruel word. How little he interested her, "with his mouth pursed like the backside of a hen over

52

the sombre mystery of his decayed teeth, the contrived and always identical disorder of his pretentious old lion's shock of hair, his grimy, chapped hands . . ."[35] The friendly Molards must have been perplexed and saddened when some time later (probably near the end of 1895) Strindberg took Ida's entirely innocent suggestion to her husband to "take the dustbin down" as an allusion to himself and, it appears, simply never returned to their home again.

At the hub of this extraordinary and brilliant circle was William Molard. Born in 1862 the son of a Mantes organist, like many of his friends he found it impossible to live off his main interest, which was music, and in consequence he had no choice but to remain at the French Ministry of Agriculture, where his clerical position earned him just sufficient to maintain the otherwise Bohemian and easy-going way of life that he had so cheerfully adopted. At home he was fond of playing his way through whole pot-pourris of Wagner operas, blithely unconcerned about wrong notes, and had a habit of stopping when he came to a chord that interested him, playing it several times over, and exclaiming, "C'est joli, ça!" Delius, Munch, Sinding and many others remembered him with affection long after the heady and diverting days that are the subject of this essay, and even Strindberg could say of him: "He is a fine man and I like him very much". He was quite handsome, rather slight in stature, with an eye for a pretty girl, something which was the cause of frequent and heated arguments in the Molard household, where "absurd accusations", as Judith Ericson-Molard remembered, would be flung about, in which Bjørnson's daughters (Bergliot?), Judith's father, telephone girls and young maidservants all occasionally figured. Judith disliked him to the bleak point of indifference. Ida Molard, a few years older than her husband, had studied at the Royal Academy of Art in Stockholm. In 1881 she had had an illegitimate daughter (Judith) by the Swedish opera singer, Fritz Arlberg. Subsequently a wealthy patron had given her sufficient funds to continue her studies in Paris, where in the event she married and settled for the rest of her life. A younger friend, Gerda Kjellberg, remembers her as "a small and extremely coquettish lady, blonde and plump, and dressed in frills and laces",[36] but in earlier days her appearance had been decidedly more eccentric and she had often affected men's clothes, smoking cigars into the

53

bargain (shades of the emancipated Scandinavian wives of Gauguin and Strindberg . . .)

The wooden house in which the Molards had their *atelier* stood in a little courtyard whose street entrance on the rue Vercingétorix bore the number six.[37] Gauguin's room was reached by a wooden staircase which saw many casual conversations between the occupant above and the Molards below. The Molards lived far from private lives, with visitors dropping in at all hours of the day, but mostly in the evenings when cheerful parties would often develop.

Gauguin's weekly 'at homes' started soon after his arrival at the beginning of 1894. He had liked the way Molard's friends had looked in on him upstairs, and started off with a little party when cakes and tea were served. This was the first of many such parties, with Judith always happy to take on the task of serving refreshments to his guests. They would all come at one time or another, Delius, Strindberg, Monfreid, Leclercq, and many others (including the painter Paul Sérusier), and Gauguin was a benign host. The adoring Judith, remembering later the secret passion she nurtured for him as a young girl wrote: "Gauguin bubbles over with an inner richness, he is the *master* overshadowing all the others, even Delius, all reduced to figuring as zeros behind this absolute" . . . "He didn't", she continues, "bear the mark of sordid poverty that was on all the artists of our milieu, both those who have succeeded since those days and those who didn't make the grade (with the exception of Delius who, obviously, is rich)".[38] Richness of course was a relative quality in this circle, and to Judith, Delius's elegant manner of dressing and the fact that he did not actually have to go out to work to make a living placed him in a special light. On the other hand Delius himself maintained that he lived "in the strictest economy". One wonders though why Judith did not include the comparatively well-heeled Daniel de Monfreid as another exception. Gauguin, too, was scarcely bothered by financial worries during the period 1894-5, thanks to an inheritance. However, Judith was not alone in her judgment. Both Richard Le Gallienne, in 1892, and Harold Bauer, a year later, had thought Delius "rich". His allowance from Delius *père* of ten pounds a month represented to Bauer "unheard-of wealth".[39]

The tone of these gatherings was often rather undergraduate, the younger Scandinavians probably helping to set the character. Released from the relatively provincial life-style that their own homelands had then to offer them, set on taking the big city by storm, cheerful, amoral, and freed from inhibitions by the readily-available bottle (Swedes, Norwegians, continuing to drink *tea* and eat cakes *chez* Gauguin?), the students simply had fun, benignly surveyed by their genial host, who would stand in front of the mantelpiece, thumb slipped into the armhole of his jacket, urbane, detached. Sometimes the company would play charades which Strindberg would almost always be the first to solve; there are memories too of Strindberg singing—out of tune—a funeral march which, according to Judith, "he alone found funny"; of Mme Schuffenecker complaining loudly of the imbecility of her husband—painfully to some, since he was there; of a Montmartre painter singing together with his wife to the strains of the guitar borrowed from their host. Inevitably, the more serious and independent-minded members of the circle, like Delius and Monfreid, for various reasons made their way less often to the rue Vercingétorix at homes as the year went on. "I don't go very much now", wrote Delius to his friend Jutta Bell-Ranske in August. "There is a man named Leclercq who I don't care for much, and he seems to have taken root there." Delius, one feels, was perhaps already in many ways 'never too close ... cautiously peering, absorbing, translating'—Whitman's words, which the composer himself was to set to music nine years later. The tall, cool and well-mannered Englishman (none of his friends in Paris ever considered him anything but exemplarily English) shared the aristocratic detachment possessed to a greater or lesser degree by his friends Gauguin and Monfreid. Like them he would not suffer fools gladly, but his essential good nature, allied to a notably developed sense of humour, restrained him from the kind of temperamental displays to which Gauguin was prone.

Gauguin had a piano in his room. Molard would sometimes go up to play, as Delius must surely have done, and one of Molard's classmates under Pessard, with whom Molard was completing his musical studies, would also occasionally play and sing there (His toneless voice was only slightly more bearable than Ravel's...). This was Léon Moreau (like Florent Schmitt a future Prix de Rome winner), who as a young composer now developed a nodding acquaintance with Delius, with the two men meeting on a number of occasions during the first half of the year. It was quite possibly

Florent Schmitt

through Moreau and early that year that Delius made another significant friendship, that of Schmitt, eight years his junior. Schmitt was as impoverished as most of the rest and was probably highly delighted to have the opportunity to make the piano reduction of *Irmelin,* on which we find him hard at work, with Delius, in May 1894. He was later to undertake the same task for

The Magic Fountain and *A Village Romeo and Juliet*. His version of *Irmelin* was not that which was ultimately published, and that of *The Magic Fountain* remains in manuscript. On the other hand his piano score of *A Village Romeo* was the basis of Delius's first private publication of the work (the later Harmonie edition of 1910 being by Otto Lindemann). Delius and Schmitt remained on warm terms for many years, although their paths were diverging by the time Schmitt wrote (in 1907 or 1908) the last of just three extant letters to his friend, since he and his wife had decided to leave Paris and live in the Pyrenees for most of the year. Delius probably helped Schmitt, when the latter went to Germany about 1902, with introductions to people who could assist him there. And it seems he had done this same service for Schmitt's visit to London shortly before; there Schmitt had met Messager, now conducting at Covent Garden, and they had talked much together about Delius.

opposite and overleaf Two pages from Ravel transcription for piano of 'Margot la Rouge'

Yet another contemporary student at Pessard's harmony classes at the Conservatoire was Maurice Ravel, and he too found his way to the rue Vercingétorix. Having just turned nineteen, he must have been among the youngest visitors on the occasion in the spring of 1894 when Molard invited a number of his classmates to meet the now celebrated Grieg at his home. Grieg was in Paris that April for a performance of one of his works and evidence points to his being together with Delius quite often then. His visit to the Molards must surely have been engineered by Delius, their intimate mutual friend. While the bright-eyed company discussed music, Ravel quietly went over to Molard's piano and began to play one of the master's Norwegian Dances. Grieg listened with a smile, but then began to show signs of impatience, suddenly getting up and saying sharply: "No, young man, not like that at all. Much more rhythm. It's a folk-dance, a peasant dance. You should see the peasants at home, with the fiddler stamping in time with the music. Play it again!"[40] And while Ravel played the little man jumped up and skipped about the room, to the astonishment of the company. Perhaps it was on a rather later occasion, when Delius was in the company of Ravel and some other French musicians, that the question was raised as to what sources modern French music was especially indebted. The French concensus view was that it was to Rameau, Couperin and Lully, etc, but Delius felt differently: "Nonsense! Modern French music is simply Grieg, plus the third act of *Tristan*". To which Ravel replied: "That is true. We are always unjust to Grieg".[41]

Florent Schmitt, incidentally, is on record as saying that William Molard's musical theories had had a considerable influence on both Ravel and himself.[42] How interesting it might prove to be if the manuscript of Molard's only known work, *Hamlet,* were one day to come to light.

Maurice Ravel

4
Scène Iᵉ
Un caffè popolare dei boulevards
È la fine della primavera. Sono le otto della sera.
Andante moderato
(alcuni bevitori seduti a un tavolino)
Totor
La Patronne
Totor

Ravel's subsequent relations with Delius are not well documented, and the French composer's biographers have all overlooked the fairly remarkable fact that in the early autumn of 1902 he transcribed for piano Delius's one-act lyric drama *Margot la Rouge,* the composition of which Delius recorded completing on June 6 that year. Incidentally, Ravel was not very keen on making a two-hand version of the Prelude: "It would have a much better effect with 4 hands", he advised Delius. The exact identity of the librettist has hitherto remained unknown. 'Paroles de Rosenval' announces the lithograph copy of the vocal score, and the signature 'Rosenval' is all that is appended to one short letter concerning *Margot* that was written to Delius in May 1907 by a Parisian woman. However there does exist in the Delius Trust Archive another letter (discussing an unnamed manuscript, copyright matters and a German translation) that was written to the composer by a Mme Berthe Gaston-Danville in September 1904, and further research has shown that both letters were in fact written by Mme Gaston-Danville.[43]

There cannot be many parallels to the labours of composers ultimately as distinguished as Schmitt and Ravel, in their transcriptions of four of a friend and fellow-composer's operas; or to the discernment that Delius showed at a fairly early stage of the development of their respective talents in leading him to commission them. Delius liked Ravel's music, much preferring it to that of Debussy, and the two men apparently remained on friendly terms for a number of years. "A bientôt, cher ami", wrote Ravel warmly in October 1902, at the close of one of his two extant letters to Delius. And in a note he sent—probably in 1909—to the pianist Theodor Szántó in Paris, he asserted: "I shall be delighted to see Delius again, whom I have not seen for years. You can count on me tomorrow at 7 o'clock."[44] Such gentle allusions as these are sufficient witness to the cordiality of their relations.

In the meantime Grieg's acquaintanceship with Molard led to a modest collaboration, with both Molard and Leclercq eagerly agreeing to translate Grieg texts into French, just as they were to do a little later with Strindberg. This work occupied some of their time in May and June 1894, and when Grieg's publisher, Dr Abraham, of the firm of Peters in Leipzig, raised difficulties regarding payment, Grieg quickly and successfully intervened on behalf of the two friends. He even prompted Delius to put in a word with Dr Abraham on their behalf: would he ask for an advance for Molard? "I think it would be welcome" wrote Grieg. "He hasn't got much to manage on". Gauguin, who had left for Pont-Aven, was hoping that the translations would give Molard the wherewithal to join him there in the summer. Grieg was delighted with the quality of the work of his two new friends and like so many others he had quickly grown to like

Molard: "He is a fine, intelligent person", he told Delius, returning to the subject in a later letter: "Molard is a very fine nature: I think highly of him as a friend and an artist".

Another composer studying in Paris in the later 1890s was Déodat de Séverac. He and Delius seemed to be on friendly terms and Delius apparently loaned him a score. In 1903 Séverac wrote a short note hoping that Delius would visit him soon so that they could talk about mutual interests, which included among other things Van Gogh and Gauguin. Their acquaintanceship however may post-date the mid-nineties by some years. Many years later, Séverac and Daniel de Monfreid, both living in the Pyrénées-Orientales, developed an intimate friendship, with Séverac composing a *Cortège catalan* to celebrate the wedding of Monfreid's daughter Agnès, and Monfreid illustrating the cover of the music.

For Delius, the early summer of 1894 saw the renewal of a friendship made some ten years earlier in Florida. Mrs Jutta Bell-Ranske, a musically gifted woman of Norwegian extraction, had lived near him during the period of his first stay in Florida, on the shores of the St Johns River. She was now in Europe, where she was to make a name for herself as a teacher of singing and voice production, and correspondence from Delius in 1894 shows her to be advising him on textual aspects of the 'lyric drama' on which he had now started work: *The Magic Fountain,* the only composition that we actually know he was creating that year. "I want to tread", he had written to her, "in Wagner's footsteps and even give something more in the right direction. For me dramatic art is almost taking the place of religion. People are sick of being preached to. But by being played to they may be worked upon". Jutta advised him on books and novels which he might read for background on the American Indians who were the subject of the work. He already had it in mind to treat of American negroes in his next stage work *(Koanga);* and Gypsies were the intended subject of a still later operatic venture.

Delius visited Bayreuth and Munich in August, and while in Munich found the opportunity to dine with Bjørnson, his wife and daughter who were staying there at the time. He heard a lot of good music during his stay and indulged a taste for beer and cigars. He seems to have missed a chance to meet Richard Strauss there, early in September: he was certainly urged on by a friend who wrote to Strauss asking him to give up to an hour to Delius.

Delius returned to Paris at the end of the first week in September but it was probably not until quite late in the year, at the Molards, that he actually met Strindberg, who had arrived in August. Little documentary evidence has been traced concerning Delius's life in the autumn of 1894. From his own short memoir on Strindberg we can construct a picture of work continuing relatively quietly at the rue

60

Ducouëdic, meals usually taken at home, an occasional lunch or dinner *chez Charlotte* in order to meet Gauguin, Strindberg and other friends. Probably not until 1895 came those long afternoon walks with Strindberg in the Luxembourg Gardens and the Latin Quarter, or perhaps to the Jardin des Plantes. Such walks *could* take an unexpected turn, for at times Strindberg would suddenly refuse to go up a particular street, feeling sure that some kind of accident or misfortune would overtake him there. A visitor to Paris later in the year was Augener, the London publisher of a number of Delius's songs, and evidence points to at least one meeting between him and Delius then. Jutta Bell-Ranske, like Bergliot Bjørnson and Emma Calvé before her, was studying with the celebrated Mme Marchesi. Perhaps she or one of her fellow-pupils introduced Delius to Marchesi, into whose orbit Harold Bauer also came. Delius frequently visited Mrs Bell-Ranske, who with her son and daughter remained in Paris for over a year, taking an apartment in the rue Morère, a mere five minutes' walk from the rue Ducouëdic.

Then there was the mysterious Princesse de Cystria (considered by some to have been a mistress of Delius's) to whom Delius was introduced by Jutta. Born in 1866, Marie-Léonie, daughter of the Duchesse de Trévise, she had married her prince in 1888, but preferred to live in Paris rather than help her husband manage his estate in far-off Guadeloupe. She enjoyed a modest reputation as a singer and enjoyed too the company of creative artists and intellectuals. Circumstantial evidence points to her securing the publication of some Delius works, most probably the five separate songs brought out in Paris by the house of L Grus *fils* in 1896. One edition of the fourth song in this series: *Plus vite mon cheval* has a dedication to her. Was she the woman who early in 1897 accompanied Delius to America, under the cloak of anonymity that left her known to Delius's American friends simply as the "Russian Princess"? This has certainly been the subject of speculation, but unfortunately the evidence is vague. We do know that in June 1896 she paid the fee for analyses by a Parisian chemist of the results of some of Strindberg's experimental attempts to make gold; the receipts for these were retained by Delius.

Then late in 1897 we find Delius writing to Jelka Rosen in Grez to say that he had an invitation card for her from "the Princess"; a month or two later, still from Paris, he passed on the news that the princess was shortly to leave the city. In May 1899 Adela Maddison wrote inviting Delius to a musical evening at her home, telling him that the Princesse de Cystria would be coming, as would Fauré and his patrons and friends the Prince and Princesse de Polignac. And the last word comes in February 1901, with Delius telling Jelka: "the princess . . . irritated me constantly with her superficial idiocy. I hope now she will leave me and my affairs alone." The papers that the Deliuses preserved from this period throw little light then on the precise nature of the composer's relations with the Princesse de Cystria.

Georgette Leblanc, wife of Maurice Maeterlinck, was another singer who admired Delius's work, although it is difficult to place a date on the one letter we have that she wrote to the composer. She had asked him to set to music a poem by Maeterlinck (to which proposal Delius had apparently agreed), and urged him to complete this for a recital of Maeterlinck's works which she was to give in a fortnight's time. However unlikely, it is tempting to think that the manuscript of yet another Delius song might perhaps be hidden among the Belgian poet's papers . . .

1895 showed a similar pattern of shared experiences with members of the Molard circle. By June *The Magic Fountain* was finished and Delius was soon casting round—in vain—for a publisher. It would be no good turning to Dr Abraham, who didn't want opera scores anyway, least of all by a continuingly unknown composer. Delius held reasonably high hopes the following year for performances of the work in Prague and in Weimar, where the score made its way; but in spite of being led to believe that his chances were good, he was ultimately disappointed—and the work remained unperformed.

But now the Delius family were growing restless about what seemed to be an absolute non-return on all the money that had for years gone into maintaining a composer whose main works stayed unperformed and unsought after. Things came to a head when Theodor resolutely refused a request from his nephew for money to help get the new opera performed, with the consequence, it seems, that uncle and nephew fell out. Financial troubles seemed likely unless a lucky break came along; and by September Delius was quite depressed and hoping that a late autumn visit to Berlin might help him sort out his musical affairs to some advantage. Gauguin, who had contracted syphilis early in the year and whose departure from France was consequently delayed as he sought treatment, had left for Tahiti, arriving there in June, and Delius and the other rue Vercingétorix friends were never to see him again; although the artist's correspondence, notably with Monfreid and Molard, was to keep the circle intermittently in touch with him during the eight remaining years of his life. Daniel de Monfreid himself spent a couple of months painting in London at the end of the year. On the whole 1895 remains poorly documented, but the creative legacy includes the completion of one opera, the beginning of another *(Koanga)*, the *Légende* for violin and orchestra, two Verlaine songs, and a start on the overture *Over the Hills and Far Away*.

CHAPTER FIVE

Jelka Rosen and the

last years in Paris

ONE JANUARY EVENING IN 1896 BROUGHT THE MOST significant meeting of all: that for the first time of Delius and his future wife. Helene ('Jelka') Rosen, a painter whose family originated in Schleswig-Holstein but who was now living (with her mother) and studying in Paris, had been invited by a friend to a dinner party. Delius was there, too, 'a tall thin man of aristocratic bearing, with dark curly hair slightly tinged with auburn, and an auburn moustache which he was perpetually twisting upwards. He wore a red tie, a memorial of earlier association with Russian revolutionaries'.[45] They talked together of mutual interests, ranging from Grieg to Nietzsche. Two days later Delius visited her, bringing a volume of his songs, for she took pleasure in singing a little, and a friendship was forged which was to result in their marriage some years later. Jelka remembered vividly the picture of Delius walking down the Avenue de Maine: "An old grey hat, his blue vivacious eyes, pale face", and how his pallor was accentuated by that red tie. He would usually be wearing his favourite coat, a McFarlane of greyish tweed, the flaps of which would invariably be thrown back over his shoulders.[46] Jelka was to bear witness to Delius's passion for taking long walks, and in the spring she often took the train with him into the countryside just outside Paris, where they would ramble through woods and lanes, sometimes returning together in the evening to his apartment where they would take a meal. After dinner Jelka would leave and Delius would begin to work. Country walks notwithstanding, Delius's nocturnalism and the noticeable pallor it induced gave Jelka cause for apprehension. "He worked most of the night, smoking and drinking red wine, stayed in bed late well into the next morning, debarred from work by the various noises in that populous and busy courtyard".[46] Strindberg too, had found the sheer din of Paris unnerving,

Portrait of Jelka Rosen by Ida Gerhardi

complaining about the "noise of trams, shouts of street-criers, rattle of trains, barrel-organs".[47] Small wonder that Delius chose to work at night.

Jelka was in love with Delius almost from the moment she met him, but the intensity of her emotion was not reciprocated by Delius, however warm the fellow-feeling and indeed affection he was to have for her. Probably not more than a year or so after he had met Jelka we find him on intimate terms with another woman. She was probably American, to judge by one or two colloquialisms in the letter she wrote to him that has somehow survived, her name was Maud, and she loved him: "I think constantly of you. We have one tremendous interest—your work. I'd make Every sacrifice toward it for you, even if it meant losing you . . . I want to see the dear eyes lose all that troubled look . . ." One other *billet doux* dates from Delius's Paris days. The signature may be 'Irma' and the message, in German, begins: "I love you with all my heart".

This was indeed a period when Delius was 'troubled'. His music stayed unplayed, financial worries lingered, his Florida farm was becoming an unwelcome liability, romantic attachments such as those with Maud and Irma might easily turn into embarrassing hindrances, and smoking and drinking through the night was scarcely the healthiest way to pass the time. And yet even when things seemed to be going badly one is already conscious of that iron will, that apparent indifference to adversity that was to become so characteristic of the man in later years.

Jutta Bell-Ranske, with whom Delius seems to have had an intellectual rather than sentimental relationship, had now moved across the English Channel and soon established herself as a teacher. Delius wrote to her in July, envying her the material success that was still eluding him: "I cannot sell a song. It seems ridiculous . . . but I cannot make a fiver". By quite early in the year he had in fact roughly sketched *Koanga,* music and libretto, and in February he sent her the libretto, inviting her comments and criticism. However, he now made the acquaintance of C. F. Keary, an English writer living at Bourron, near Fontainebleau, and confided the rewriting of the text to him. "My literature", he acknowledged to Jutta, "is not on a level with my music".

Delius's ripening friendship with the splendid Daniel de Monfreid is another feature of this period, each visiting the other as the mood—or invitation—took him. The Monfreids were now living in one of a pretty cluster of low-roofed studios set a little back from the Boulevard Arago in a thickly-planted garden, and Delius had already got to know one or two of his friend's neighbours there. On 18 March 1896 he was invited to lunch, by the Monfreids, in the company of the poet Le Rouge, and the convivial occasion was prolonged when they all decided to drop in on Sterner next door, where they found a crowd of people. Two days later, Monfreid provides in his diary the first record of Delius's friendship with Edvard Munch. It was probably at Delius's suggestion that Munch then paid a first and unexpected call on the Monfreids, who were just settling down to lunch. Daniel was obviously taken with the newcomer, as he repaid the call in two days' time. On the last day of the month Delius went along to the *Vernissage* of the *Salon des Indépendants*. Monfreid had called in the morning to give him an invitation, and among their friends there that afternoon were the Molards and the Schuffeneckers. Delius shortly returned the favour, giving Monfreid a ticket for a concert in Paris on 14 April. Just before this he had paid a short visit to Bourron, presumably to confer with Keary on the subject of the new opera.

Some eight years later Monfreid reminisced nostalgically about these times "when you used to have us up to your little apartment at Montrouge, round the table for a cup of your good old steaming 'Tara Tea' . . . We too, my dear friend, keep the same warm feelings for you, just as keen and just as sincere, because they come from a community of ideas and of feelings, a similarity of tastes and of appreciation of art and the things of life."

"I am together with Delius and Vilhelm Krag by day", wrote Edvard Munch on 27 March 1896. "They both live near me—the Latin Quarter as it's called".[48] Munch is the last of Delius's friends during the Paris period who can be discussed here in any detail. This was to become perhaps the most tightly-knit and durable friendship of all those that Delius enjoyed with creative artists during this

Edvard Munch:
Self-portrait (detail)

time. Just two years younger than Delius, Munch had come from a similar background, although his cultured middle-class parents had none of the financial substance enjoyed by Delius's family. On the contrary they were no strangers to financial difficulties. By now Munch knew Paris well. He had first come there for a few weeks in 1885; we find him again in the city in the autumn of 1889, together with two artist friends. One cannot discount the faint possibility of his having met Delius then, remembering Delius's already substantial acquaintance with a number of Norwegians in Paris. Later came winter visits to Nice and Monte-Carlo, where Munch, in his turn, contrived 'infallible' systems for the gaming-house. Then followed, around 1892, a lengthy stay in Berlin, where he moved into the *Zum Schwarzen Ferkel* café circle, which included Strindberg, Stanislaw Przybyszewski, Christian Krohg, Adolf Paul and Richard Dehmel. Holger Drachmann and Gunnar Heiberg were also introduced into this circle, all of whose members, according to one account, seemed to be driven by "sex, art and alcohol". Munch's relationship even then with Strindberg was tempestuous and when their acquaintance was resumed in Paris it was moodily coloured by Strindberg's precarious mental balance. Delius himself tells of one occasion, in the summer of 1896, when he and Munch paid a short and entirely amicable call on Strindberg in his rooms in the rue d'Assas, [49] while the Swede was busily engaged on his scientific experiments. After they had left, Strindberg decided that Munch had intended to assassinate him, and a postcard which reached Munch the following morning informed him that the attempt had failed. The paths of Strindberg and Delius now diverged anyway, with Strindberg returning to Sweden in the summer, and neither saw the other again.

Munch was conscious that in spite of his comparative celebrity—or notoriety—in Germany by now, he was virtually unknown in France, and he knew, as did so many other painters at this time, that he needed to make a name for himself in Paris if he was really to succeed as an artist. Delius recognised this too, and few people can have done more for Munch than he did during the next few years, advising the artist, helping to arrange exhibitions of his work, suggesting prices for his pictures, all with the dedication of a friend who had realised that here was a major talent to be assisted and promoted in every possible way.

In the summer Delius was in Norway again and back at work on *Koanga*. He sent a song to Grieg (probably one of the two Verlaine pieces composed the previous year), and the older man found it "very impressive", adding, with a hint of disapproval at the eroticism he discerned in it: "But how very French you have become!" December saw Delius in Bradford, looking back on the completion of a *Romance* for cello and piano, and further work on *Koanga* as well as, possibly, on his 'fantasy overture' *Over the Hills and Far Away*. Nothing seemed to have come of the two operatic works he had so far completed. One score *(Irmelin?)* he had taken in September to Karlsruhe; the General Music Director, Felix Mottl, was "very interested" but found neither the work nor (more pointedly) the libretto fully to his taste. However, he asked Delius to let him know if anyone else were to take it on, as he would like to attend the première. Delius was at a crossroads in his life. *Koanga* was halfway to completion. He was delighted at the way it was shaping and determined to get it performed in London. (Ironically it was not to be

67

fully staged in that city until 1935, a year after his death). He was now quite seriously considering moving to London, having probably realised that he would get no further in Paris, at least in hearing his music performed, and therefore being eager to till new ground rather closer to home. He had also recently completed an *American Rhapsody* (a first version of his *Appalachia),* and first indications in Bradford were that he might get it performed there before long. "The bigger and better orchestras of England are unreachable for me at present and I have neither wish nor energy enough to go kicking around the ante-chambers of well known Conductors and as I feel quite certain that one of these days they will be kicking their heels in my ante chamber I give myself no trouble about them".[50] Johannes Wolff was, it seems, to perform his *Légende* in London in January, and he himself was to leave that month for Florida once more, intent on seeing what personal advantage it might yet be possible to secure from the orange grove he had earlier farmed and to which his father still possessed the title. He was accompanied on the trip by his Norwegian friend Jebe, with whom he had spent some time in Norway the previous summer, and by the 'Princess' who had simply followed him onto the ship, only disclosing her presence to Delius when they were well out to sea.

In the event he did return to Paris, in the early summer of 1897. Learning that Jelka Rosen had with her mother's help purchased the house at Grez-sur-Loing that he had first seen a year ago in her company, he made his way to the quiet village that was effectively to be his home for the rest of his life. In a sense this means that post-1896 Paris is really an epilogue to this account, a prelude to the years of more settled maturity at Grez. Delius was for some years to retain rooms in Paris; and Jelka herself confessed that he would leave Grez for days, or even weeks, that would be spent in Paris with other friends, other women, in his old haunts. His contracting of syphilis possibly dates from about this time. He certainly knew a number of Paris's brothels; and he was, it seems, particularly attracted to oriental girls. The letters of Halfdan Jebe that have survived convey some of this information to us, even if they tell us considerably more about Jebe and his own racy life-style, with its elements of high talent, gleeful vulgarity and sheer bawdy good humour. On one occasion Delius was commended for knowing how "to skim the cream off the milk and to pluck the flower of youth". An intriguing letter Jebe sent to Delius in 1904 shows the Norwegian's continuing interest in his friend's adventures: "You went to Paris, just for a few days, but what days. How immoral." Jebe's moral influence could by no stretch of the imagination be demonstrated to be beneficial to Delius—whatever the pair's excellent artistic responses to each other—for on an earlier occasion we find him inviting Delius to join him in a hashish "orgy" in Paris. It is scarcely surprising then that Jelka actively tried to drive a wedge between the two men.

The summer of 1897 seems largely to have been spent at Grez. Gunnar Heiberg, the Norwegian dramatist, was one of Delius's visitors during this period, and plans were laid for Delius to compose incidental music for Heiberg's play, *Folkeraadet,* which was to receive its première in Christiania in the late autumn. Heiberg found Grez a "paradise", and thoughts of living in London or elsewhere must have been receding from Delius's mind as he considered his good fortune. In Jelka he had found a devoted companion who loved both the man and his music; added to this she now owned a pleasant, airy house with a garden of great beauty falling gently away to the banks of the peaceful river Loing. The village in which this haven was set was itself tranquil and charming, and still remained a haunt of artists. Some years before, Carl Larsson and Karl Nordström were painting there, and their fellow-countryman Strindberg had based a part of his *Among French Peasants* on Grez and its surroundings, which he knew well. Robert Louis Stevenson and his cousin Bob had been visitors to the village; so had Corot, followed by the American artists Will Low and Francis Brooks Chadwick, the latter having elected to settle there and continue painting. John Lavery made several visits to Grez over the latter years of the nineteenth century and painted a number of views of the bridge, as did almost all the artists who adopted the village, not excluding Jelka. Roderic O'Conor, too, would come to see the Chadwicks and to paint. And there were many more. The summer mecca would be the Chevillon, an inn just beyond the bridge, with a riverside garden; and the villagers were sufficiently inured by now to artists and their strange ways for few eyebrows to be raised on account of the nude bathing that took place in the river there. All in all Grez was an agreeable, stimulating and often unconventional place in which to live.

Portrait of Fritz Delius
by Christian Krohg

When Delius set off for Christiania and *Folkeraadet* in October, his Parisian friends kept their fingers crossed for him: "Delius has just left for Norway to supervise the performance of one of his works—We all wish him every success", wrote Molard to his (and Leclercq's) friend Gabriel Randon.[51] They were not to realise that this particular event, in spite of the temporary notoriety it conferred on Delius in Norway (nationalist feeling and his setting of the Norwegian national anthem in a minor key were the essence of the trouble—and a blank shot was fired at the conductor, Per Winge) was of far less significance than a scarcely-noticed first performance the following month of his *Over the Hills and Far Away*. This was given by Hans Haym, conductor at Elberfeld, in Germany, to whom Delius had recently had an introduction through Jelka's painter friend, Ida Gerhardi. Haym's initial recognition of an exceptional talent and his subsequent promotion of Delius's music laid the ground for Delius's growing fame in Germany in the early 1900s.

The year had been productive, in spite of Delius's long absences in the United States and in Norway. *Over the Hills and Far Away* and *Koanga* were completed, although the latter had to wait until 1904 until it was first produced in a stage version, in Elberfeld. The first version of the piano concerto had been penned in the early Floridian spring. And as well as the *Folkeraadet* music, Delius had written his *Seven Danish Songs* (with orchestral or piano accompaniment). Perhaps his achievement in at last getting two of his works publicly performed within a short space of time helped ease family difficulties. At any rate we know that by early 1898 there was a reconciliation with his uncle—perhaps fortunately, for Theodor died shortly afterwards and left his nephew an appreciable sum of money.

Will Molard was delighted with Delius's achievement in Christiania and a little later wrote to Munch, who was now back in Norway: "Since we last saw each other you will have met in Christiania friends from our circle—Leclercq and Delius—the latter has certainly had a real success in Norway and has kept the newspapers rather busy; this has been fortunate for him, because at any rate attention has now been drawn to Delius's name up there and this can never do any harm."[52]

Some of the correspondence of Gauguin, Monfreid and Molard during the years of Gauguin's self-exile has been preserved and, supplemented by Monfreid's diaries, helps to round out the picture. One member of the circle, Charles Morice, collaborating with Gauguin on *Noa-Noa*, was planning in the autumn to draw from Gauguin's story "a sort of lyric pantomime or *'ballet doré'* ". Molard, he felt, would be the obvious composer for the work (no mention of Delius). Nothing however seems to have resulted from this chance for Molard to achieve the breakthrough of which he wistfully dreamed. Then Monfreid recalls how on one October afternoon in 1898 Delius, the Molards, Gilles Gérard (who was to marry Judith), and Achille Ouvré all called on him at his new home in the rue Liancourt. This is the first evidence of Delius's friendship with Ouvré, a gifted artist then 36 years of age. He exhibited frequently at the *Salon d'Automne* and at the *Indépendants,* and executed many portraits of musicians and writers. Of particular interest to us are his portraits of Delius, Molard, Ravel ('all angles, like his music', as one critic aptly wrote) and Theodor Szántó, who was to become a noted exponent of Delius's piano concerto. Much later, in the summer of 1913, a letter Ouvré wrote to a friend almost certainly refers to another Delius than that of the Paris period: "I have taken the opportunity to plan a . . . cycle trip with a friend to Grez-s-Loing where we intend to drag a smile from a good old misanthropist friend of ours who affects to enjoy himself there all the year round".[53]

Early in November 1898, having learnt of the forthcoming legacy from his late uncle Theodor, Delius, together with an unidentified "Norwegian lady", called on Daniel de Monfreid and from among the Gauguin canvases that Monfreid had recently received from Tahiti decided to buy *Nevermore,* for the sum of 500 francs. He was, incidentally, to invest a far larger proportion of his inheritance in the huge concert of his own works that he sponsored in London the following May. The two men went off together to deliver the canvas to a framer, and Monfreid wrote to Gauguin to inform him of the sale: "The second cheque is the price that Delius, our English friend, offers you for one of your best works: "Nevermore", the woman lying on the bed with a yellow fabric under her head. He can't give you more than 500 francs for it; but knowing that you wanted to put this canvas by to sell at a high price, I only let him have it on condition. If the amount seems too low to you, he'll let you have it back for the price he paid for it . . . However I think I did well to let him have this fine piece; for it will be seen by the *very numerous* well-connected people cultivated by Delius".[54]

A few days later Delius called again on Monfreid to hand him the money for the frame, a further fifty francs. Gauguin replied the following January: "You did well to let Delius have the picture "Nevermore". He pays more than Vollard . . . You remember you reproached me for having given a title to this picture; don't you think that the title *Nevermore* is the reason for this purchase—Perhaps! Whatever the case, I'm very glad that Delius is its owner, seeing that it isn't a speculative purchase to resell it, but bought because he likes it; then some other time he'll want another, especially if callers compliment him on it or get him to talk about the subject".[55]

Monfreid was reassured: "I'm glad that you don't disapprove of the sale to Delius", he replied. "As a matter of fact he's a lad who likes your painting, and especially this canvas. Not because of the title: he told me that himself. But because it's a *beautiful painting.* An opinion with which I completely agree".[56]

Before long the house at Grez was to have an enviable collection of the works of friends. Not only was there the Gauguin, but works by Munch, Rodin and Monfreid among others. There were Jelka's paintings too. And indeed it was *through* Jelka that the friendship with Rodin was established, a friendship that added yet another shaft of colour to the spectrum of Delius's artistic interests.[57]

Delius in 1899

CHAPTER SIX

Farewell to Paris

DELIUS'S EFFECTIVE CONTACT WITH THE MOLARD circle was diminishing now that he was mainly at Grez. As its members grew older, anyway, they tended to leave Paris. Strindberg and Gauguin had gone. Leclercq was shortly to die, Boutet de Monvel to marry and settle in the country. Daniel de Monfreid moved to the family home in the Pyrenees. Slewinski was tucked away in Brittany, where he stayed, except for a long absence in Poland, for the rest of his life. Mucha was looking for wider fields to conquer, America in particular. Munch had returned to Norway. In fact only the Molards, of the principal members of the group, were to remain faithful to Paris until they died (Ida in 1927 and William ten years later).

There *were* other notables who made a habit of calling at the Molards' home: composers such as Maurice Alquier and Omer Lethorey; and writers like Guillaume Apollinaire and Alfred Jarry, who were for a time 'regulars' at the rue Vercingétorix, bringing in their train yet another painter Henri (le Douanier) Rousseau. Delius would sometimes attend the Sunday evening at homes of the Douanier, according to Osbert Sitwell, who met the composer for the first time many years later. "He was the one Englishman I have ever met," remarked Sitwell, "who knew personally the giants of the Post-Impressionist Movement, recognised them for what they were, and was privileged to frequent their studios."[58]

In the early 1900s, Delius's meetings with the Molards were growing rather sporadic, but letters from William in 1902 and 1908 show that Delius was ever ready to lend a helping hand in musical matters, trying in the first instance to place with a publisher an article Molard had written on *Pelléas and Mélisande,* and in the second arranging for Thomas Beecham to meet him in Paris. Beecham's intention to visit the rue Vercingétorix in 1908 is recorded, as is

Molard's eager expectation that the English conductor would study the score of his "Shakespearian elucubration" *Hamlet*—and indeed play it. Ouvré went to London in June especially to hear Molard's music, but reported to Delius: "comme d'habitude, cela a raté." Molard's last extant letter to Delius, dated 23 December 1908, conveys thanks for Beecham's address: "I have just asked him to send back my scores so that I can present them again to Chevillard." At Delius's request he also sent Ravel's present address in Paris.

There is little to suggest that Delius's music has ever had a real chance in Paris. Certainly, his songs and chamber works were occasionally privately performed. For example Fauré and "a few of the best young French musicians" played through *Koanga* at the Paris home of Adela Maddison one spring afternoon in 1899. Among those present were the Prince and Princesse de Polignac and a few other musical people: "I think I may say they were quite enthusiastic", wrote Delius. And on one public occasion Claude Debussy, no less, was the acid reviewer in *La Revue Blanche* of a performance of the *Danish Songs* for soprano and orchestra, translated into French by Molard and given at the Société Nationale on 16 March 1901, under Vincent d'Indy's baton. As a critic Debussy's tone of mocking irony could be directed at almost any composer—Wagner, Richard Strauss, Saint-Saëns—and for just one occasion Delius was the target: the *'Poèmes Danois'* were 'very sweet songs, very pale, music to lull convalescent ladies to sleep in the rich quarters'.[59] For the record Delius never heard a note of Debussy's *Pelléas* until after he had completed his own operatic masterpiece *A Village Romeo and Juliet*. The subject matter and treatment of the latter bears intriguing similarities to Debussy's interpretation of a tale of star-crossed, tragic young love, yet each work was born and bred quite independently. Delius greatly admired Debussy's opera: "Pelléas and Mélisande is *exquisite*—the best thing I have seen for years, full of poetry and delicacy".

Delius certainly did not take kindly to one suggestion that he perhaps borrowed from both Debussy and Puccini: "I am not the sort of man", he wrote, "who would deny his musical parentage, and . . . the first note I ever heard of Debussy was his opera, 'Pelléas and Mélisande', in the spring of 1902 in Paris. My work, 'Romeo und Julia auf dem Dorfe', was thus entirely finished, and since three months in Rome, in the hands of Florent Schmitt (a Prix de Rome), who did the piano score. I have never yet heard a note of Puccini's music. The resemblance with Debussy can come from both of us being influenced by Chopin, Wagner, and a little by Grieg."[60] Reinforcing the point on a later occasion when speaking of Debussy and Ravel, Delius told his friend Percy Grainger: "We are *contemporains* but I have not been influenced by them." Whether

74

Grieg's influence on Delius has been over-emphasised in the past is not a subject for these pages, but a prominent and well-informed acquaintance of both men, Robin Legge—himself a fellow-student of Delius and friend of Grieg in Leipzig days—'never credited' such influence. He went so far as to advance in 1929 the rather startling theory that it was more possible that Delius, always 'a law unto himself' and much the more powerful personality, exerted influence over Grieg.[61] Maybe the obvious comparison—the piano concertos—should be discounted if the idea is to be taken with any seriousness . . . But Legge pointed out that Grieg spent the winter of 1887-8 in Leipzig (and incidentally a great deal of time in the company of Delius) precisely 'to "learn" modern orchestration' under Hans Sitt. He was certainly delighted with his stay: "When I think of how lucky I have been in my associates this winter . . . I can say with good reason that my journey was worth while."[62] Above all, Grieg admired his younger friend's songs; the scores of the *Five Songs from the Norwegian* had stood open "for months", as he told Delius, during the summer of 1888 on his piano. One passage in *Longing,* to words by Kjerulf, he added, "I just cannot forget, and will show you one day that I can steal after all."

French criticisms of Delius are hard to come by, perhaps not surprisingly considering the little attention given to his music in the French-speaking countries. Two critics writing in French in the early years of the century, Robert d'Humières[63] and William Ritter (a Swiss),[64] gave favourable notices in French journals of the premières in Germany of *A Village Romeo and Juliet* (Berlin 1907) and *A Mass of Life* (Munich 1908—although the work was not given in its entirety). D'Humières had in fact translated for Delius the *Village Romeo* libretto into French some years earlier, and his review could scarcely have been expected to be impartial. But on the whole the pages of French musical publications have remained resolutely closed to Delius's life and music. Even when, as late as 1968, a brave and favourable essay on the composer was written in French, it was in a journal published in Brussels, and not in Paris, that it inevitably and almost perversely had to appear.[65]

The composition in 1899 of Delius's orchestral showpiece *Paris,* subtitled *The Song of a Great City,* may now be seen as a valedictory gesture to the city and to that whole rich period he had spent in it, perhaps even as a nostalgic farewell to youth. Delius called the work a nocturne, and the score is suffused with the magic of a Parisian night, from the first pages, conjuring up an impression of the Seine shrouded in mist, through glittering passages evoking the city's streets, cafés and cabarets, to the cool dawn of a new day. Delius prefaced his full score of the work—which appears still not to have been performed in the city which inspired it—with the following lines:

Mysterious city—
City of pleasures,
Of gay music and dancing,
Of painted and beautiful women—
Wondrous city,
Unveiling but to those who,
Shunning day,
Live through the night
And return home
To the sound of awakening streets
And the rising dawn. [66]

How much of Delius's own experience is encapsulated in these few lines, unremarkable as they are in themselves. The Parisian interlude—extensive both in terms of time as of artistic experience and development—was virtually over. Paris had not been conquered by his music, but he had left his mark there indelibly, in the minds and memoirs of men such as Gauguin, Munch, Mucha and so many others whose words have helped fill out this account. Now followed the years of stability and compositional maturity at Grez-sur-Loing, where nearly all his greatest works were to be written. And as he turned to England and to Germany for the success which had eluded him in France, Paris became a diversion which was on the whole easily resisted. The city was henceforth to play little part in a creative life which was to be dominated by the will to compose in tranquillity. For Delius, youth and an epoch had come to an end.

Notes
and
Sources

NOTES

1   Letter to Grieg from Delius at St-Malo, 19 October, 1888.

2   *Breve fra Edvard Grieg til Frants Beyer, 1872-1907.* Ed. Marie Beyer. Steenske Forlag, Kristiania, 1923. p 86-7.

3   Recorded by Percy Grainger during the course of conversations with Delius in April 1927 (Mss in the possession of the Grainger Museum, Melbourne University, Australia).

4   This *Paa Vidderne* is quite distinct from the accompanying music Delius wrote in 1888 to Ibsen's long poem and which bears the same name.

5   Bjørnson, Bjørnstjerne: *Aulestad Breve til Bergliot Ibsen.* Gyldendalske Boghandel, Nordisk Forlag, Kristiania & Copenhagen, 1911. p 151.

6   Beecham: *Frederick Delius,* p 79.

7   Confirmed in a letter to the author (19 October 1973) from John Hickey, one of Delius's executors, now living in Nice. Le Gallienne's original letter is no longer to hand.

8   Egan, Richard Whittington (& Smerdon, Geoffrey): *The Quest of the Golden Boy. The Life and Letters of Richard Le Gallienne.* Unicorn Press, London, 1960. p 187-8.

9   One letter only from Arvesen is preserved. Writing from Norway on 2 August 1907 he regretfully declares that he cannot at the moment afford the relatively modest 4500 francs Delius is asking for his violin. Delius had probably given him first refusal.

10 Bauer, Harold: *Harold Bauer: his book.* Norton, New York, 1948. p 59-60.

11 Buffen, F: *Musical Celebrities* (2nd Series), Chapman and Hall, London, 1893. p 108.

12 Calvé, Emma: *Sous tous les ciels j'ai chanté.* Plon, Paris 1940. p 185-6.

13 Encausse, Philippe: *Papus (Vie,* p 77).

14 Encausse, Philippe: *Papus (Oeuvre,* p 5).

15 *La Revue des Revues,* 9, 4. Paris, 1 October 1894. p 72.

16 Vollard, Ambroise: *Souvenirs d'un Marchand de Tableaux.* Éditions Albin Michel, Paris 1937. p 107.

17 Heseltine seems in 1923 to have been the first of Delius's biographers to record the date of this concert as 1893, since when it has not been corrected.

18 Tardieu, Eugène: 'Paul Gauguin', *Écho de Paris,* Paris, 13 May 1895.

19 Mette Gauguin to Émile Schuffenecker, 15 September 1893.

20 Gauguin to Émile Schuffenecker; cf. Danielsson, *Gauguin,* p 40.

21 Gauguin, Paul: *Intimate Journals,* p 50.

22 Gauguin to Mette Gauguin, March 1892.

23 Gauguin to Molard, 16 March 1902.

24 Monfreid to Gauguin, 1902; cf. Loize: *Les Amitiés du peintre Georges-Daniel de Monfreid*. p 74.

25 Monfreid to Gauguin, September 1901; cf. Loize, *op cit,* p 74.

26 Gauguin to Dr. Gouzer, 15 March 1898. The Musée d'Art Moderne, in Paris, has a number of Monfreid's paintings, and others may be seen at the Musée Toulouse-Lautrec, in Albi. It was of course in 1893 that Monfreid executed his sensitive pastel study of Delius at the piano.

27 Gauguin to Molard, 16 March 1902.

28 Wildenstein *Catalogue* nos. 386 and 507 respectively.

29 Mucha, Jiri: *Alphonse Mucha*, p 91.

30 Bibliothèque Nationale, Paris (Papiers Jehan Rictus, *Nouvelles acquisitions françaises* 24564).

31 Bibl. Nat., *ibid.* ff 620-1.

32 Strindberg to Adolf Paul, 26 May 1894; cf. Sprinchorn: Introduction to *Inferno,* etc, p 46.

33 From *Inferno;* quoted in Freda Strindberg: *Marriage with Genius,* p 400. Other quotations from letters Strindberg wrote to his wife are also taken from Freda Strindberg's book.

34 *Inferno,* quoted in Söderström: *Strindberg och bildkonsten.* p 277.

35 Kjellberg, Gerda: *Hänt och sant,* p 63.

36 Danielsson, *op cit,* p 149.

37 The sudden and calamitous development of Montparnasse has only just obliterated all traces of this side of the street. Nothing remains. At the time of writing, a similar homely, old-fashioned group of *ateliers* (No. 3, on the other side of the road), still lived in, takes on a ghostly quality as it waits its turn to become rubble for the foundations of further huge glass and concrete blocks.

38 Kjellberg, *op cit,* p 54.

39 Bauer, *op cit,* p 59.

40 Gérard-Arlberg, Gilles: 'Nr 6, rue Vercingétorix', p 65.

41 Conversations with Delius: Grainger Papers, University of Melbourne. Also recorded, in slightly variant form, in Grainger's 'The Personality of Frederick Delius', *The Australian Musical News,* 1 July 1934 (*vide* p 14).

42 Gérard-Arlberg: 'Nr 6, rue Vercingétorix', p 67.

43 Internal evidence and certain similarities in the handwriting of the two letters (although two quite different pens were used) were recently noted: it seemed likely that both were from the hand of one and the same writer. Then a seductive clue appeared in the manuscript collection of the Bibliothèque Nationale, in the form of a letter written by the novelist Gaston Danville which contains a reference to a certain Karl Rosenval (*Nouvelles acquisitions françaises* 24553, f 475). Examination of the General Catalogue

of Printed Books in the Bibliothèque Nationale revealed that Gaston Danville was the *nom de plume* of Armand Blocq, and further enquiry showed that in the Fonds Spécial de l'Histoire de France in that same library there was preserved a notification of the marriage in Toul (Lorraine), on 24 May 1893, of Armand Blocq and Berthe Kahn-Rosenwald. The marriage was a Jewish one, and Germanic origins may be postulated for one if not both of the families involved. In the wake of the Franco-Prussian War and the annexation of Alsace-Lorraine it is perhaps not surprising to find a comparative gallicising of names such as Rosenwald to Rosenval.

The link between Delius and his future librettist was undoubtedly forged in the context of the Molard circle, for it was on 9 December 1893 and to Gabriel Randon that Gaston Danville addressed the letter mentioning Karl Rosenval. And Randon (who was better known under his own *nom de plume* of Jehan Rictus!) was an intimate friend of Molard and Leclercq. In 1897 Delius himself subscribed to an elegant edition of Randon/Rictus' *Les Soliloques du Pauvre*. On the composer's relations with the Gaston Danvilles before 1902, the date of *Margot,* nothing however has yet come to light —perhaps not surprisingly considering the welter of pseudonyms that have until now served to cloud the issue.

44 This note is in the collection of the Library of Congress, USA. I am grateful to Mr. Arbie Orenstein of the Music Department of Queen's College, New York, for drawing my attention to it.

45 Beecham, *op cit,* p 77.

46 *Ibid,* p 80.

47 Letter to Freda Strindberg, *op cit,* p 344.

48 Letter from Edvard Munch to his aunt, Karen Bjølstad, in *Edvard Munchs Brev: Familien* (ed Inger Munch). Munch-Museets Skrifter, 1. Oslo 1949.

49 Not the rue d'Arras, as often misquoted.

50 Frederick Delius, Bradford, to Jutta Bell-Ranske, December 1896. Coll. Jacksonville University Library, Florida.

51 Bibl. Nat. (Papiers Jehan Rictus, *Nouvelles acquisitions françaises* 22, ff 13-14. Correspondance de Molard.) Munch's teacher, Christian Krohg, an artist and journalist of distinction, came to sketch and interview Delius after the concert for his paper *Verdens Gang.*

52 Munch Museum Archive, Oslo.

53 Achille Ouvré to Clément Janin, 11 June 1913 (Bibliothèque d'Art et d'Archéologie, Paris, Cartons 79/80.)

54 Monfreid to Gauguin, 11 November 1898.

55 Gauguin to Monfreid, 12 January 1899.

56 Monfreid to Gauguin, 11 March 1899.

57 Cf. Carley, L: 'Jelka Rosen Delius: Artist, admirer and friend of Rodin. The Correspondence 1900-1914'. *Nottingham French Studies,* 9, 1 and 2, 1970.

58 Sitwell, Osbert: *Great Morning: An Autobiography.* Macmillan, London 1948. p 252.

59 *La Revue Blanche,* 24, 188. Paris, 1 April 1901, p 551.

60 Spanuth, August: 'A New Musical Dramatist', *The New Music Review,* 6, May 1907. I have not seen a copy of this article but am indebted to William Randel for the quotation.

61 Legge, Robin: 'World of Music. Delius Festival', in *The Daily Telegraph,* 12 October 1929.

62 Monrad-Johansen, David: *Edvard Grieg,* p 282.

63 'Une première à l'Opéra-Comique de Berlin. Frédéric Delius.—Roméo et Juliette au village.' *Bulletin de la S.I.M.,* 3,3. 15 March 1907. p 324-5.

64 Concert review in *Le Courrier Musical,* Paris, 1908, p 434.

65 Ackere, Jules van: 'Un musicien méconnu: Frederick Delius, coloriste.' *Revue générale belge,* Brussels, May, 1968.

66 As quoted by Felix Aprahamian in notes for Delius Festival programme, 4 November 1946.

PRINCIPAL WORKS CONSULTED

(Books are published in London unless otherwise stated)

Ahlström, Stellan: *Strindbergs Erövring av Paris*. Stockholm Studies in History of Literature, No. 2. Stockholm, 1956.

Augé-Laribé, Michel: *André Messager: Musicien de Théâtre*. Paris, La Colombe, Éditions du Vieux Colombier, 1951.

Beecham, Sir Thomas: *Frederick Delius*. Hutchinson, 1959.

Brunet-Moret, Jean (& Jamin, Armand): *Ville d'Avray et son histoire*. Ville d'Avray, La Municipalité, 1970.

Calvé, Emma: *My Life*. New York and London, Appleton, 1922.

Catinat, Jacques: *C'est arrivé à Croissy*. Paris. Éditions S.O.S.P., 1970.

Danielsson, Bengt: *Gauguin in the South Seas*. Translated by Reginald Spink. Allen and Unwin, 1965.

Delius, Clare: *Memories of My Brother*. Ivor Nicholson and Watson, 1935.

Delius et Papus: *Anatomie et Physiologie de l'Orchestre*. Paris, Chamuel 1894.

Delius, Frederick: 'Recollections of Strindberg'. *The Sackbut, 1, 8*, December 1920 (p 353-4).

Encausse, Philippe: *Papus, Dr. Gérard Encausse, sa vie, son oeuvre*. Paris, 1932.

Fenby, Eric: *Delius as I Knew Him*. Bell, 1936.

Ferroud, P.O.: *Autour de Florent Schmitt*. Paris, Durand, 1927.

Gauguin, Paul: *Intimate Journals*. Translated by Van Wyck Brooks, Heinemann, 1930.

Gauguin, Paul: *Lettres de Gauguin à sa femme et à ses amis*. Ed. Maurice Malingue. Paris, Grasset, 1946.

Gauguin, Paul: *Lettres de Paul Gauguin à Georges-Daniel de Monfreid*. Éditions Georges Crès et Cie, Paris, 1918. (New edition, ed. Annie Joly-Segalen. Paris, Falaize, 1950).

Gérard-Arlberg, Gilles: 'Nr 6, rue Vercingétorix'. *Konstrevy*, (Stockholm), 35, 2, 1958 (p 64-8).

Hemmings, F. W. J.: *Culture and Society in France 1848-1898*. Batsford, 1971.

Heseltine, Philip: *Frederick Delius*. John Lane, The Bodley Head, 1923 (Reprinted with additional material, 1952).

Jahoda, Gloria: *The Road to Samarkand: Frederick Delius and His Music*. New York, Scribner's, 1969.

Jaworska, Wladyslawa: *Gauguin and the Pont-Aven School*. Translated by Patrick Evans. Thames and Hudson, 1972.

Jefferson, Alan: *Delius*. Dent, 1972.

Kjellberg, Gerda: *Hänt och sant*. [including memoirs of Judith Gérard] Stockholm, Norstedts, 1951.

Lara, Isidore de: *Many Tales of Many Cities*. Hutchinson, n.d.

Leclercq, Julien: *La physionomie, d'après les principes d'Eugène Ledos*. Paris, Larousse, 1896.

Leclercq, Julien: *Le caractère et la main, histoire et documents*. Paris, F. Juven, n.d.

Leclercq, Julien: *Strophes d'amant*. Paris, Alphonse Lemerre, 1891.

Loize, Jean: *De Maillol et Codet à Segalen—Les Amitiés du peintre Georges-Daniel de Monfreid et ses reliques de Gauguin*. Chez Jean Loize, 1951.

Lowe, Rachel: *A Catalogue of the Music Archive of the Delius Trust, London*. Delius Trust, 1974.

Monfreid, Georges-Daniel de: *Carnets*. Unpublished diaries in the possession of Mme Annie Joly-Segalen, Paris.

Monrad-Johansen, David: *Edvard Grieg*. Translated by Madge Robertson. New York, Tudor, 1945.

Mucha, Jiri: *Alphonse Mucha: His Life and Art*. Heinemann, 1966.

Nectoux, Jean-Michel: *Fauré*. Paris, Éditions du Seuil, 1972.

Roland-Manuel: *Maurice Ravel*. Translated by Cynthia Jolly. Dennis Dobson, 1947.

Smith, John Boulton: 'Portrait of a Friendship: Edvard Munch and Frederick Delius'. *Apollo*. January, 1966 (p 38-47).

Söderström, Göran: *Strindberg och bildkonsten*. Forum [Sweden], 1972.

Sprigge, Elizabeth: *The Strange Life of August Strindberg*. Hamish Hamilton, 1949.

Stang, Nic.: *Edvard Munch*. Translated by Carl J. Knudsen. Oslo. Johan Grundt Tanum Forlag, 1972.

Stenersen, Rolf: *Edvard Munch. Naerbilde av et geni*. Oslo. Gyldendal Norsk Forlag, 1946.

Strindberg, August: *Inferno, Alone and Other Writings*. In new translations. Edited and introduced by Evert Sprinchorn. New York, Doubleday, 1968.

Strindberg, Freda: *Marriage with Genius*. Cape, 1937.

Wildenstein, Georges: *Gauguin: I. Catalogue*. Paris, Les Beaux-Arts, 1964.

Appendix

Two unpublished songs

Chanson [de] Fortunio, to words by Alfred de Musset, exists in an autograph manuscript inscribed by the composer *Croissy le 12 Novembre 1889.* *Nuages,* a setting of a poem by Jean Richepin, exists in an autograph manuscript dated by the composer 1893. Both manuscripts are in the Delius Trust Archive, where they form part of a group of songs bound into Delius Trust Volume 36 (ff 37-38 and 39-40 respectively).

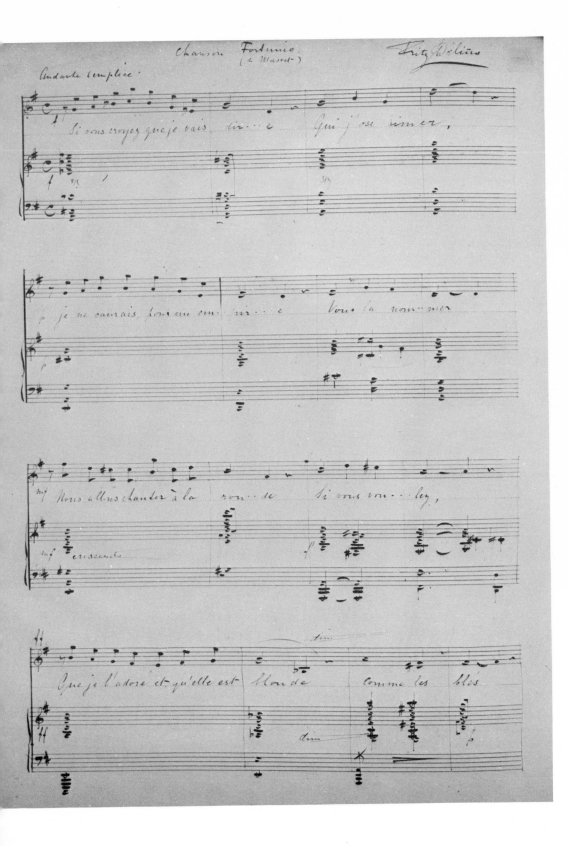

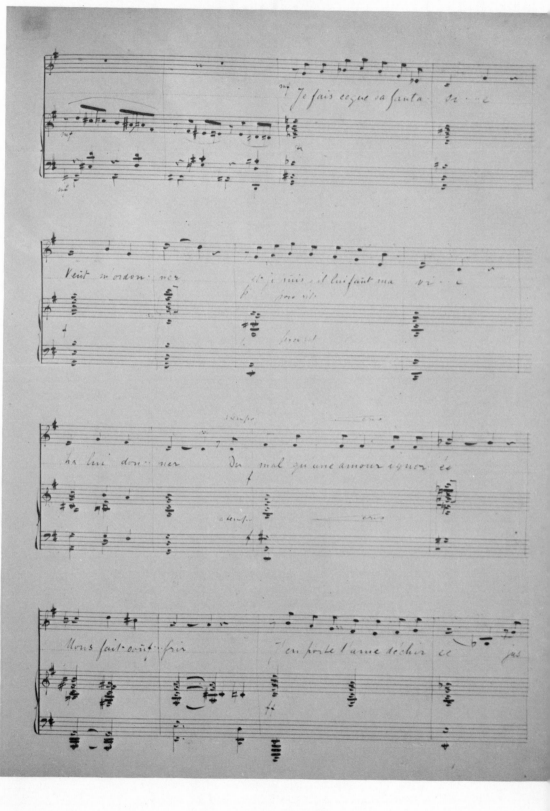

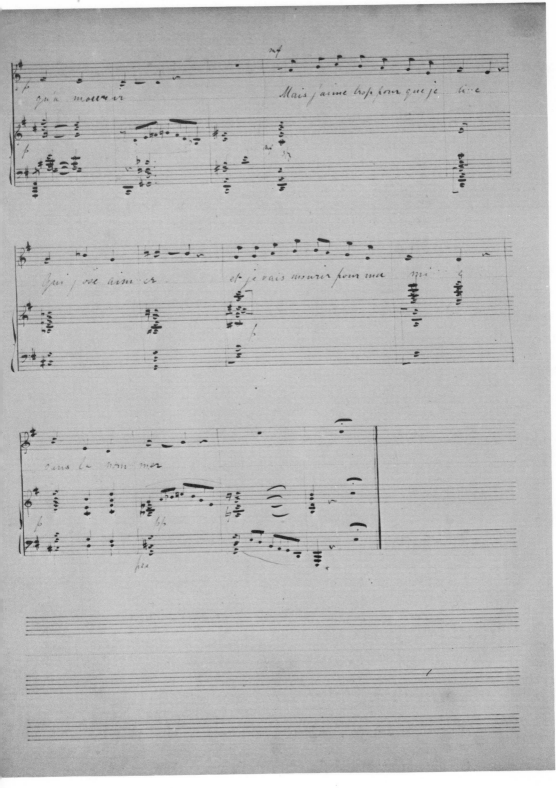

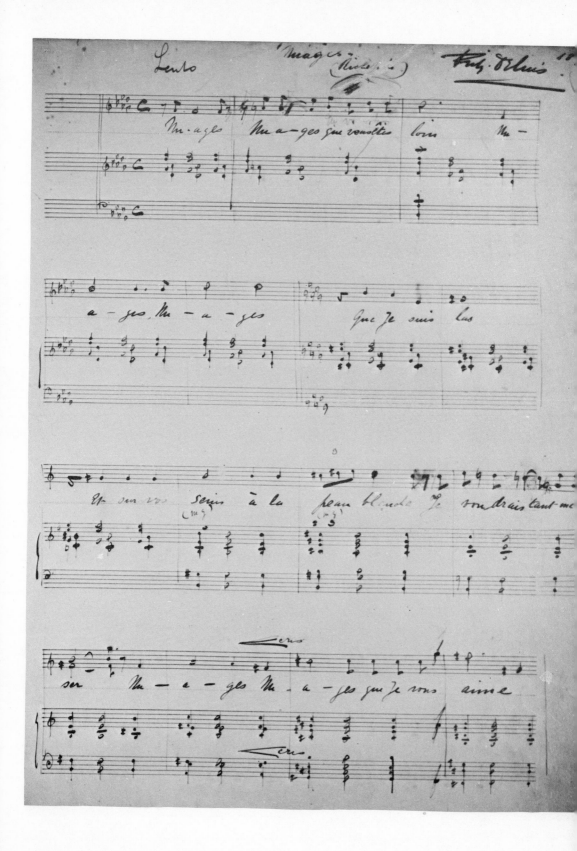

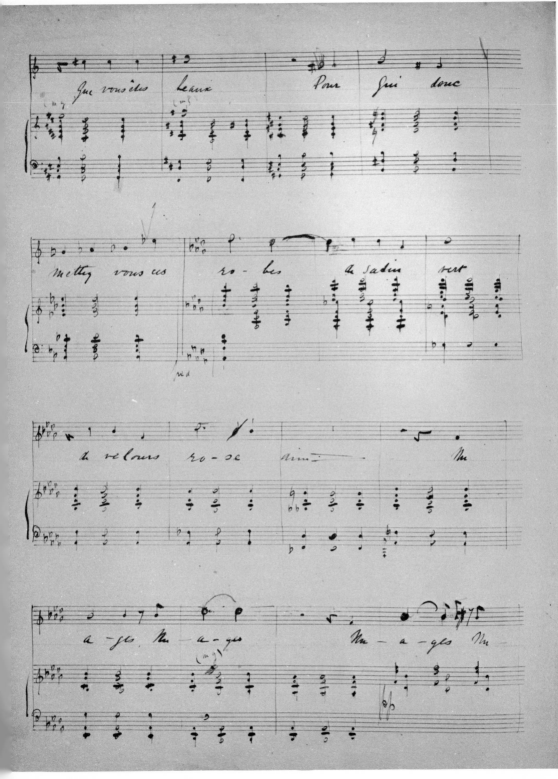

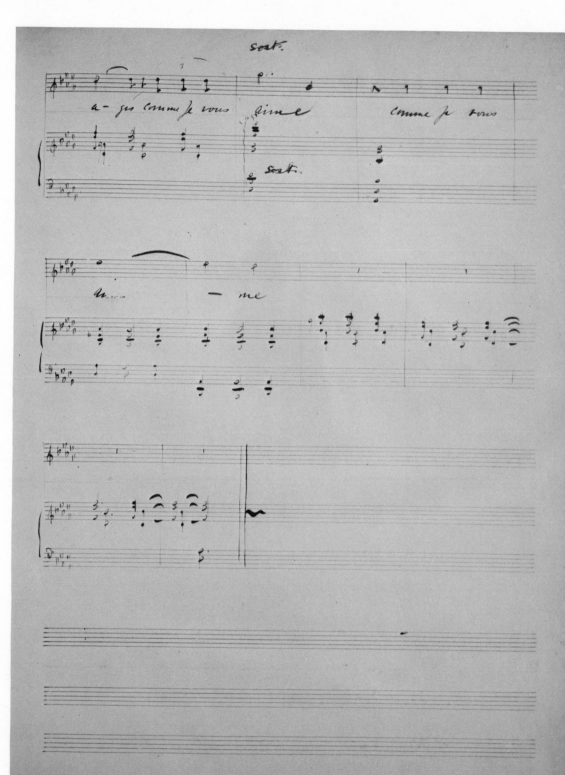

INDEX

Delius's works, including arrangements, are entered in the alphabetical sequence in *italic*. Works by other composers are entered under the name of the relevant composer and indented. The Introduction, Notes and illustrations are not indexed.

94

Of this book published by

TRIAD PRESS
10E Prior Bolton Street
CANONBURY
London N1
England

Six hundred copies have
been printed
of which this is number

353

Designed by Lewis Foreman

Set in English 49

and printed by

Howard Jones Associates
SWANSEA
Wales.

6 rue Vercingétorix